MW01630535

*This guide is dedicated to the amazing CM and VM
of Team Adventure. I couldn't be more proud of you both.*

Always brave. Ever, ever, ever.

Forever in my heart - Dad

Disclaimer:

The Pokémon Scarlet and Pokémon Violet are registered trademarks of The Pokémon Company. The screenshots and artwork shown in this publication were taken from "Pokémon Scarlet" and/or "Pokémon Violet", games developed by GameFreak and published by Nintendo.

This educational guide is a 100% independent and unofficial publication which is in no way, licensed, authorized, or endorsed by The Pokémon Company or Nintendo. This guide book is for general information and entertainment purposes only.

Names, brands, and logos mentioned within this publication may be protected by trademark or other intellectual property rights of one or more jurisdictions. It is not implied that there is any commercial, or other relationship, between the publisher and the trademark holder.

This strategy guide's text and layout is Copyright © 2023 by Alpha Strategy Guides.

All rights reserved.

No part of this book may be reproduced in any form, or by electronic or mechanical means, including information storage and retrieval systems, without the expressed written permission from the author ("Alpha Strategy Guides"), except for the use of brief quotations in a book review.

Table of Contents

Introduction
Welcome to Paldea...

Welcome to our guide to the latest release in the amazing series that is Pokémon.

It goes without saying that Scarlet and Violet are extremely enjoyable games that embrace the open world design and *finally* give you the freedom to explore the world at your leisure - and in whatever order you want.

Creating a *helpful* guide for an open world game is always an interesting challenge.

One one hand, it's important to get you the help you need, whilst also not trying to push you down a specific path of our choosing.

Which is interesting in Scarlet and Violet as the designers *have* a "preferred" path that they want you to follow (the main story-line missions have a natural path to follow where the Pokémon you encounter all become ever so slightly tougher).

So, we've tried to strike a balance between giving you the details you need to conquer those gyms, titans, and crew's like a pro, while also advising you of the "preferred path" (should you find yourself struggling against an over-powered opponent).

We also do our best to uncover the game's coolest secrets, and a provide a whole lot more info for your benefit.

We hope you find our guide to your time in Paldea a helpful and enjoyable companion to have by your side. It's certainly been an adventure in itself to put it together for you.

Warmest regards,

Alpha Strategy Guides

What's New?

What makes it different

Pokémon Scarlet and Violet are the culmination of Game Freak's long-term vision of a Pokémon game where you can now explore a true open world, tackle gyms in any order you choose, play against other Pokémon trainers online around the world, and just enjoy battling and capturing all-new Pokémon (along with a large handful of fan-favorites).

And while it *may* be somewhat "rough around the edges", it's also a very rewarding and enjoyable game, filled with everything that many millions of Pokémon fans have been wanting for *years*.

As before, each colored version includes some exclusive Pokémon that you can then trade with someone who owns the other version of the game.

It also features a whole new feature where you can power-up your Pokémon with new types (that are completely different from its natural type(s), adding a whole new tactical element as new strengths (and weaknesses) are made available.

You can also jump online and have up to three other friends join you as you run around the world, battling other Pokémon - while trying to catch'em all!

There's also three separate mainline stories that you can jump in and out of (but you'll need to finish all three to gain access to the end-game and post-game content).

Finally, you can send your Pokémon out to fight wild Pokémon beside you, earning the whole team EXP!

Finally, you can craft special sandwiches and chill out with your Pokémon at picnics, taking selfies and doing other cool activities!

There's *a lot* to do, so let's get to it!

Orthworm, the Lurking Steel Titan
Union Circle
Tera Raid Battle
Link Trade
Surprise Trade
Link Battle
Battle Stadium
Mystery Gift
Online
Try your hand at Tera Raid Battles.
News

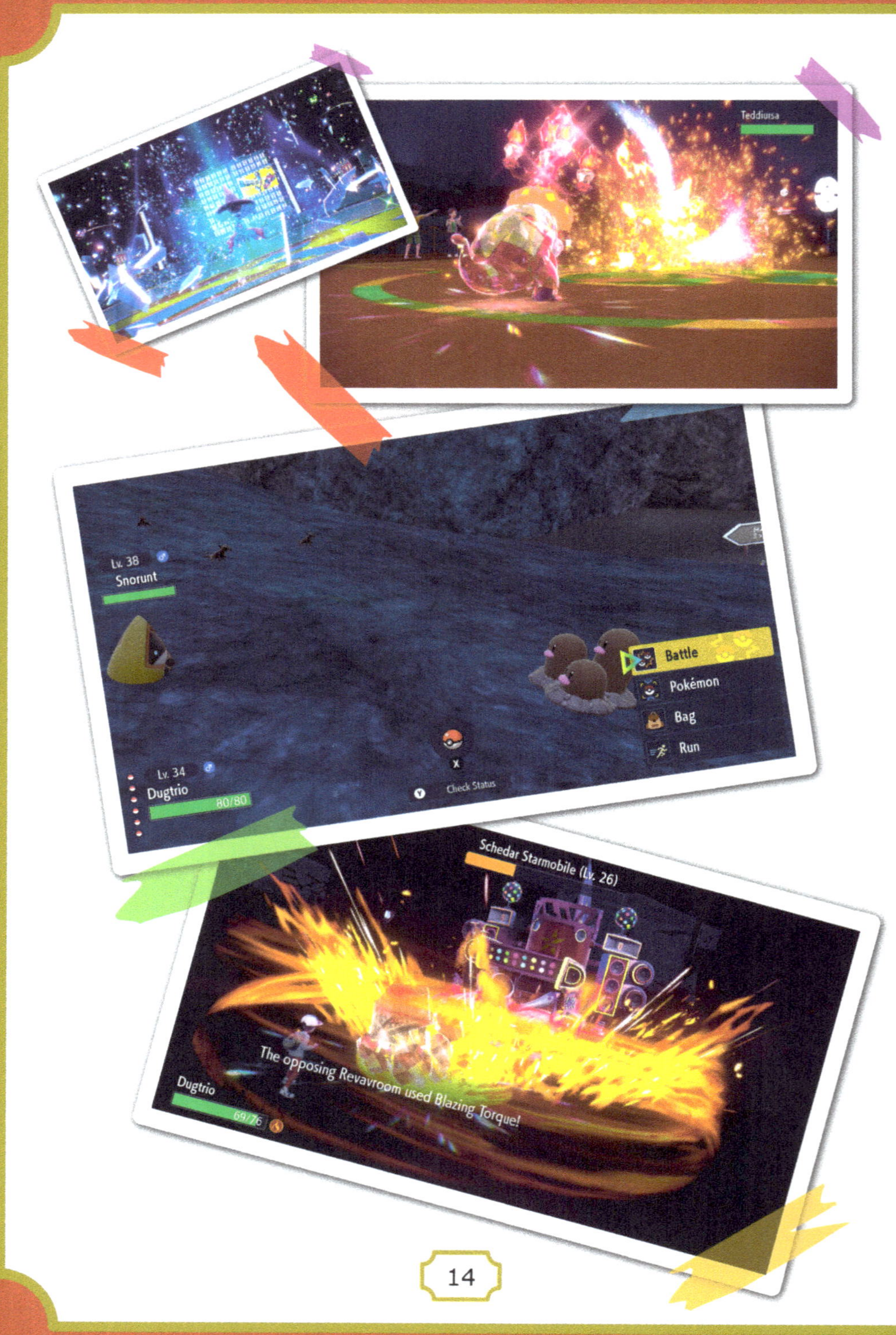
Teddiursa
Lv. 38
Snorunt
Battle
Pokémon
Bag
Run
Check Status
Lv. 34
Dugtrio
80/80
Schedar Starmobile (Lv. 26)
The opposing Revavroom used Blazing Torque!
Dugtrio
69/76

Battles
And how they work

If you're new to the franchise, then it's important to understand how the battle system works in Pokémon.

You can battle against either Pokémon that are walking out in the world "aka: in the wild", or in a set battle against other Pokémon Trainers (or Gym Leaders).

However, if you're looking to catch a particular Pokémon to add it to your ever-growing collection (which is one of the biggest reasons so many players play Pokémon in the first place), then you can *only* catch those that you battle in the wild.

You **cannot** catch a Trainer's Pokémon (only merely defeat it and make it "faint").

The Battles

Pokémon uses a "turn-based" approach, so take your time to pick and choose what move you wish to use..

Not all attacks are designed to cause damage as some are designed to either increase (or decrease) a key stat.

Each Pokémon has its own set of "stats" (such as Speed, Attack level, Special Attack level, and more).

And these stats play a role in *who* gets to attack first, whether or not they have a special "buff" that automatically impacts them (or a different Pokémon entirely).

To make things even more interesting, a key element of battles in Pokémon centers around the fact they all Pokémon are of a certain "type" (some are also made of two types - known as "Dual Types").

This is the corner-stone of battles in the series, so let's take a closer look at how that all works out…

Types

Each Pokémon belongs to one or more types, such as **Fire**, **Water**, or **Electric** (to name just three). These types determine which moves are effective against which Pokémon, and also affect the outcome of battles. Each type has its own strengths and weaknesses.

For example, **Fire-type** Pokémon are strong against **Grass-types**, but weak against **Water-types**. Similarly, **Electric-types** are strong against **Water-types**, but are weak against **Ground-types**.

Each type also has a neutral relationship with some types and are not affected by them.

When two Pokémon of different types battle, certain moves will be super effective (i.e. deal more damage) against the opposing Pokémon, while others won't be very effective (i.e. deal less damage).

Knowing the strengths and weaknesses of different types is an important part of strategy in the game, as it allows players to select the most effective Pokémon and moves for each battle.

We've compiled a quick-reference guide on how much damage (if any) are dealt between the different types of Pokémon.

You can find that handy chart on the next page.

Dual-Types

We cover this aspect in more technical detail in our **Battle Chart** section on *page 22*.

However, in a nutshell, Pokémon that have two different types will inherit the strengths *and* weaknesses to both types.

Take *Pawmo* for example. It's primarily an **Electric-type**. However, it's *also* a **Fighting-type**, meaning that it can use **Fighting-type** moves that make it Super Effective at battling a further **five** types!

Segin Starmobile (Lv. 20)
Arm Thrust
Super effective   18/20
Nuzzle
Effective   20/20
Spark
Effective   20/20
Quick Attack
Effective   30/30
Lv. 26
Pawmo   50/77
Move Info
Can Battle
PSYCHIC   FAIRY
FAIRY
Status
Type
Tera Type
Hypnosis   20/20
Draining Kiss   10/10
Teleport   20/20
Psybeam   20/20
Super effective
Has no effect
Synchronize
Ability
If the Pokémon is burned, paralyzed, or poisoned by
another Pokémon, that Pokémon will be inflicted with
the same status condition.
Back
Pawmo   4/ 77   Lv. 26
Kirlia   53/ 53   Lv. 21
Tauros   57/ 57   Lv. 17
Fletchinder   76/ 76   Lv. 28
Crocalor   98/ 98   Lv. 30
Dugtrio   70/ 70   Lv. 29
Koraidon
Orthworm, the Lurking Steel Titan
It's super effective!

Oh no!
The Pokémon broke free!

Leveling up

It's also important to keep in mind what level your Pokémon team are at, and also what the average level the Pokémon around you are likely to be.

As a general rule of thumb, the further north you go on the map, the higher the level of wild Pokémon you're most likely to encounter.

Go in too high and even average moves can be powerful (which is annoying when you want to catch them and end up making them all faint!).

While it's entirely possible to capture a Pokémon that's of a higher level than anyone else on your team, they may refuse to listen to your battle commands!!!

The only way to make sure that a Pokémon of a certain level **will** listen to you is by beating the right number of Gym leaders. Each one you beat opens up another five or more levels that listen to you.

Only once you beat every gym leader in the **Victory Road** story-line will *any* level of Wild Pokémon listen to you!

Finally, leveling up a Pokémon also opens up new moves for it to learn.

To Catch or to Defeat?

If you're fighting a Pokémon in the wild, then you need to decide whether or not you want to try and catch it (or just defeat it for the EXP).

If you want to try and catch it, then you'll - ideally - want its health as low as possible (think: "In the red zone").

If its health isn't low enough (or, its level is much higher than yours), then there's a good chance it'll break free from the Poké Ball you used (wasting that Poké Ball)!

Afflicting it with a status ailment beforehand (e.g. paralysis or sleep) makes it easier.

Be sure to heal any Pokémon caught as their status is-as you caught it!

The cornerstone of any successful Pokémon battle is the ability to know which type(s) are super-effective against other types.

Going into a battle with the right type of Pokémon in your team will mean the difference between one-shotting an opponent (because your move caused 2 - 4x damage), versus using a move that only did ½ damage - or worse *zero* damage (because your opponent was immune to that type of attack).

While we cover all of the main story-led battles in our guide, we can't realistically cover *every* *single* minor battle that you can come up against.

And that's where our at-a-glance battle chart comes in.

We've tried to keep the chart as simple-to-read as possible, allowing you to quickly gauge what type of move will not only deal the most damage (found on the right-side of the next page) but we also show you what types of moves will cause *your* Pokémon to take the most damage (found on the left side of the next page).

Another critical aspect to keep in mind is that there's often Dual-Type Pokémon around.

Got a move that deals 2x damage to one of the types, but only 0.5x to the second type? Multiply the 2 x 0.5 and your move now only hurts it 1x (making it neutral).

However, if *both* attacks happen to deal 2x damage each type (of the Dual-Type Pokémon), then 2x2 = 4x the damage caused!

Caution

This isn't 100% guaranteed (as there's many other factors in play - such as held items and TT form). However, it'll help you loads against *most* wild Pokémon.!

To use the chart below, begin on the left-side ("Your Attack Type") and then go right and look up at the type of Pokémon you want to battle ("Their Pokémon Type") to see how much damage that move will do.

Damage Multiplier	Effect Attack Type Has
0	"Has no Effect" (Zero damage)
0.5	"Not very effective" (1/2 damage)
2	"Super Effective" (2x damage)
Note: An empty box means the move causes 1x damage.	

Their Pokémon Type

Your Attack Type (rows) vs. Their Pokémon Type (columns):

Your Attack ↓ / Their →	Bug	Dark	Dragon	Electric	Fairy	Fighting	Fire	Flying	Ghost	Grass	Ground	Ice	Normal	Poison	Psychic	Rock	Steel	Water
Bug		2			0.5	0.5	0.5			2				0.5	2	0.5	0.5	
Dark		0.5			0.5	0.5			2						2			
Dragon			2		0												0.5	
Electric			0.5	0.5				2		0.5	0							2
Fairy		0.5	2			2	0.5		2					0.5				
Fighting	0.5	2			0.5			0.5	0			2	2	0.5	0.5	2	2	
Fire	2		0.5				0.5			2		2				0.5	2	0.5
Flying	2			0.5		2				2						0.5	0.5	
Ghost		0.5							2				0		2			
Grass			0.5				0.5	0.5		0.5	2			0.5		2	0.5	2
Ground	0.5			2			2	0		0.5				2		2	2	
Ice			2				0.5	2		2	2	0.5					0.5	0.5
Normal									0							0.5	0.5	
Poison					2				0.5	2	0.5			0.5		0.5	0	
Psychic		0				2								2	0.5		0.5	
Rock	2					0.5	2	2			0.5	2					0.5	
Steel				0.5	2		0.5					2				2	0.5	0.5
Water			0.5				2			0.5	2					2		0.5

Skiddo Leaf   × 1
Kilowattrel defeated
a Mudbray!
Mudbray Mud   × 1
Kilowattrel
Lv. 28   +85
Houndour
Lv. 20   +42
Pawmo
Lv. 26   +42
Pikachu
Lv. 12   +42
Petilil
Lv. 13   +42
Clodsire
Lv. 27   +42
09:08
13/30
Dugtrio
Clodsire
Clodsire defeated
a Houndour!
Buizel defeated
a Houndour!

Autobattles
Let's Go!

By using the new 'Let's Go!' feature, it's now possible to send **one** of your Pokémon out by themselves into the Paldea region. Press **ZR** to send your main Pokémon out into the big world to battle.

You can also manually send it in the direction you're facing by pressing **R** when it's not in a battle.

Once they're out exploring on their own, they can automatically battle other nearby Pokémon.

For every battle that they win like this, the experience points are automatically shared between the current active team (up to six Pokémon). The higher the level of opponent defeated, the more EXP there is to share around the team.

The main Pokémon gets double everyone else, but the rest still get some and it's an *amazing* way to passively increase the levels of multiple different Pokémon at the same time (without needing you to manually fight single battles).

You'll also earn a load of items that can be used for creating new TMs at Pokémon Centers.

Note

It's important to keep in mind that, if you set a Pokémon off and it takes too much damage, it'll come running back to you before finishing that battle.

You'll then need to take it to a Pokémon Center for healing, or use an item from your bag on it.

Caution

You *cannot* catch any wild Pokémon while using "Let's Go", all defeated opponents faint by default.

POKÉ PORTAL
Online Mode
Union Circle
Tera Raid Battle
Link Trade
Surprise Trade
Link Battle
Battle Stadium
Mystery Gift
Try your hand at Tera Raid Battles.
News
Back

Multiplayer
Local co-op or Online Play

It's been a long time coming, but you can now enjoy the first true open-world Pokémon game with up to four other players at once!

Join up with up to four friends (or strangers) and trade Pokémon, battle each others Pokémon, take on Tera Pokémon together, or even just stand back, watch, and encourage them as they explore the world.

The Union Circle

Found within the Poké Portal, the Union Circle is where you want to go to setup your multiplayer session.

Trading Pokémon

There's two ways to trade Pokémon in S&V.

1. Link Trades

2. Surprise Trades

Link Trades

Use this option to trade Pokémon with a specific person (such as a friend).

Surprise Trades

A surprise trade lets you pick which Pokémon you want to trade before the game picks a random trainer (located elsewhere in the world) to trade your Pokémon with.

The perfect feature for finding the Pokémon that you need to complete that Pokédex once and for all!

Tera Types
Gem-like Pokémon

Pokémon S&V introduces the concept known as the "Terastallize Phenomenon." Think of this as the equivalent to the Mega Evolution, Z-Moves, or Dynamax found in previous generations.

What does it do exactly?

This new feature allows Pokémon who Terastallizes to shine and glimmer like a gemstone, while also enhancing the strength (or changing the weakness) of the affected Pokémon.

Every Pokémon type has a Tera form that it can take on, but the actual form is inactive until the Pokémon terastallizes while in battle (but you can see what it is before using it).

For example, some Eevee's will have a Normal Tera Type, other Eevee's will have a Flying Tera Type! There's 18-types to keep an eye out for - that's a lot of combinations! Rare Tera Types also exist. Keep an eye out!

How to Terastallize Your Pokémon

Firstly, you must have a **Tera Orb**. Once you have one in your possession, you can activate it on any Pokémon and the Tera Orb will now be unavailable to re-use until it has recharged.

They can be recharged by either touching Terastal Energy Crystals, or by visiting a Pokémon Center.

However, only a single Pokémon can be Terrastallized during battle and they will remain in the form until the battle has ended.

Note

If Pokémon Tera Type matches that of the original type, then you'll be granted an extra increase in attacking power (STAB)!

The Rarer Tera Types

One of the easier ways to encounter the rarer Tera Types of Pokémon is to go look for shining crystals as they trigger off Tera Raid Battles (they're accompanied by a large pillar of bright light - they're easy to spot).

Note

The color of the shining crystal match the Tera Type of the Tera Pokémon waiting inside.

Thankfully, you can wait for other trainers (local or online) to join you as you defeat the Tera Pokémon inside within a set time limit, or challenge it by yourself.

Caution

You can only take in one Pokémon with you to battle - so pick carefully!

One of the cool things about this team battle is that there's no waiting for other trainers to take their turn.

Therefore, it's essential that you - very quickly! - learn how to co-operate with your fellow trainers.

Cheer Them to Strength!

Believe it or not, but cheering on your Pokémon can raise one of its stats! There's three types of cheers that you can use and the following stats affected are:

- Boosted Attack + Sp. Atk,

- Boosted Def + Sp. Def,

- Healing.

What's even better, is that anyone can use these cheers! Which makes playing together even more enjoyable and a pleasant team-like experience.

Be Sure to Catch Them!

Deplete their health before the timer expires (and without all of your team's Pokémon being rendered unconscious), you can take a chance at catching it.

And it's definitely worth doing, as you'll not only catch a rare Tera Type, but everyone also gets a bunch of other rewards for their help! Sweet!

Crocalor
53/ 70
Lv. 21
Fletchinder
51/ 51
Lv. 18
Diglett
38/ 38
Lv. 19
Gimmighoul
37/ 37
Lv. 13
Maschiff
45/ 45
Lv. 16
Pawmi
48/ 48
Koraidon
MAIN MENU
Bag
Boxes
Picnic
Poké Portal
Options
Save
You saved your progress!

Petilil
Sandile!
Sand Tomb!
Eli
Kirlia!
Confusion!

The list of TMs you can make at
TM Machine has been updated!
Flash Cannon
thers all its light energy and releases it at
the target's Sp. Def stat.

Special Tera Raid Battles!

If your Switch is connected to the internet, then keep your eyes open for special events. These events will be automatically downloaded to the Poké Portal News (where any special Tera Raid Battles can be found), or you can do this manually by using the *Mystery Gift* menu option.

The following information pertains to post-game content. We've kept this as spoiler-free as possible!

Black Crystal Tera Raids

Once you've finished the main story-line, you're presented with the opportunity to take on some really formidable opponents who are substantially tougher than regular Tera Types!

For example, between the 1st - 4th and 15th - 18th December 2022, *Charizard* appeared inside a Black Crystal for you to battle and then capture.

What makes these events extra special is the fact that Nintendo may bestow them with additional prizes for beating them.

For example, if you can capture the *Charizard* mentioned (while it's available), then you will have a special **Dragon** Tera Type imbued with the very rare **Mightiest**.

It's worth bearing in mind that you may only be able to catch *one* of each type of Black Crystal Tera Type Pokémon per save file.

Now, while the Black Crystals are formally reserved as post-game challenges, it *is* possible (although *highly* discouraged) to join the post-game Black Crystal Tera Raid of another trainer at the start.

However, it should go without saying that wading into such a high-level battle with a "less than stellar" Pokémon will - most likely - result in your Pokémon being KO'd in a matter of seconds. Consider yourself well and truly warned!

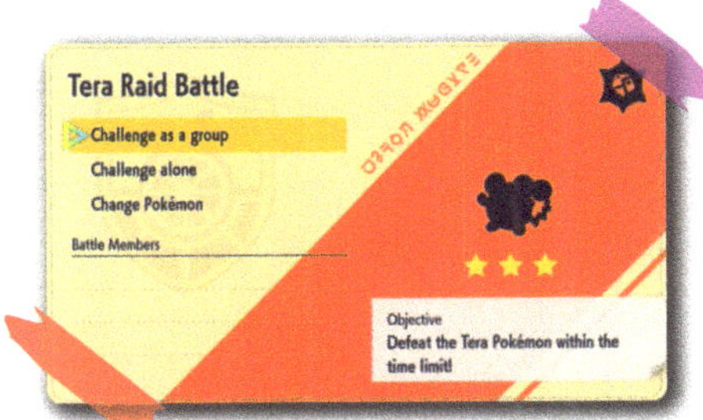

Picnics
Relax with your friends

Picnics are new and allow you to do so all sorts of really cool things while you and your Pokémon chill-out together. Let's take a closer look at the reasons why you should make the most of this new feature…

1. Where and why?

You can set up a picnic almost anywhere. You can even customize your furniture and other picnic items to your tastes!

Once you set up your picnic, all of your active Pokémon come out to play together (including your chosen Legendary)!

2. Be a Sandwich Master

Combine ingredients and build your sandwich of choice in this new mini-game. Take care not to knock your sandwich all over the table!

Each sandwich grants a unique affect (along with restoring that Pokémon's HP). What will you make?

3. Forge bonds (and find eggs!)

Not only will your Pokémon interact with each other as they relax and play, but this is the only way to breed Pokémon in S&V!

4. Clean your Pokémon!

Your lovely Pokémon can now become dirty as they battle or traverse across the map with you.

Giving them a good scrub not only strengthen their bond with you, but it also restores their HP again. Very handy!

5. Enjoy them with friends!

Set up picnics with up to three other friends when playing via the Union Circle!

You can join other players in their world, show off your Pokémon, and watch them all interact.

You can make sandwiches together, take group photos, watch everyone's Pokémon play together - and maybe even find Pokémon eggs!

6. Stats-boosting Meals

Food now plays a role in helping you to achieve specific tasks. Need to catch a particular type of Pokémon? There's a meal for that.

Want to boost the odds of finding a rare Shiny Pokémon? There's a meal for that too!

Meals can be bought in restaurants across the various towns, or they can be made by you as sandwiches (which we cover in more detail on the next page).

Meals can also come in different levels (the higher the level, the bigger the boost).

Top Tip!

Meals only last for 30-minutes. That's it. One thing you can do to maximize its use is to disable the auto-save feature and *then* save the game manually just before you eat the meal.

If you didn't get the result you wanted (such as catching that shiny), then simply reset the game and try again!

Let's take a closer look at what meals do what…

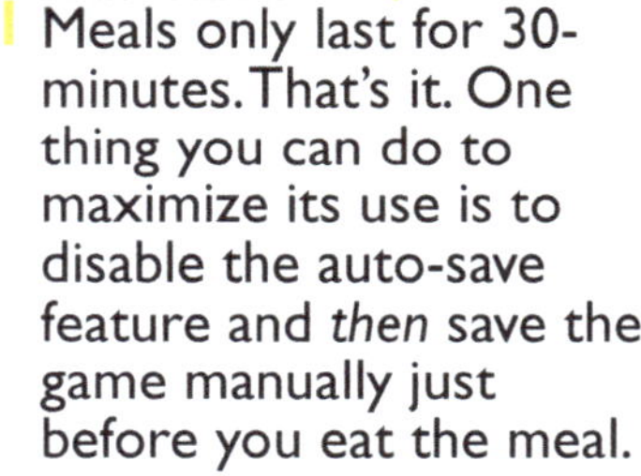

Meal Powers

Meal	What the Power does
Egg Power	Increased odds of finding Pokémon eggs in the picnic basket.
Catching Power	Increased odds of catching Pokémon with Poké Balls.
Exp. Point Power	Increased amount of EXP from battles.
Item Drop Power	Increased amount of TM materials from battles.
Raid Power	Increase the amount of rewards earned from winning Tera Raid Battles.
Title Power	Increased odds of finding Pokémon with Titles.
Sparkling Power	Increase the odds of running into *wild* Shiny Pokémon only.
Humungo Power	Increased odds of running into larger Pokémon.
Teensy Power	Increased odds of running into smaller Pokémon.
Encounter Power	Increased odds of running into Pokémon of a specific Type (useful when trying to catch low spawn-rate types of Pokémon).

Restaurant Meals

Meal	Name	Cost	Meal Power
	Zesty Sandwich	1750	Humungo Power: Psychic Lv. 1 Exp. Point Power: Fighting Lv. 1 Encounter Power: Water Lv. 1
	Jam Sandwich	850	Catching Power: Fighting Lv. 1 Item Drop Power: Psychic Lv. 1 Egg Power Lv. 1
	Tropical Sandwich	1450	Egg Power Lv. 1 Encounter Power: Fighting Lv. 1 Catching Power: Dragon Lv. 1
	Marmalade Sandwich	950	Item Drop Power: Fighting Lv. 1 Catching Power: Rock Lv. 1 Egg Power Lv. 1
	Avocado Sandwich	1200	Exp. Point Power: Dragon Lv. 1 Encounter Power: Electric Lv. 1 Catching Power: Dark Lv. 1
	Paella de Paldea	1800	Humungo Power: Dark Lv. 1 Egg Power Lv. 1 Item Drop Power: Water Lv. 1
	Fruit Punch	950	Catching Power: Psychic Lv. 1 Encounter Power: Fairy Lv. 1 Teensy Power: Water Lv. 1
	Escalivada	1500	Raid Power: Ice Lv. 1 Encounter Power: Dragon Lv. 1 Exp. Point Power: Psychic Lv. 1
	Potato Tortilla	1600	Item Drop Power: Poison Lv. 1 Humungo Power: Grass Lv. 1 Egg Power Lv. 1

Meal	Name	Cost	Meal Power
	Klawf al Ajillo	1500	Encounter Power: Electric Lv. 1 Exp. Point Power: Rock Lv. 1 Raid Power: Fairy Lv. 1
	Seafood Pinchos	1500	Encounter Power: Water Lv. 1 Raid Power: Dark Lv. 1 Exp. Point Power: Ghost Lv. 1
	Arroz con Leche	950	Item Drop Power: Steel Lv. 1 Catching Power: Grass Lv. 1 Humungo Power: Ground Lv. 1
	Ceviche	1300	Humungo Power: Bug Lv. 1 Exp. Point Power: Fighting Lv. 1 Item Drop Power: Ground Lv. 1
	Smoked Fillet with Herbs	1400	Egg Power Lv. 1 Teensy Power: Ghost Lv. 1 Exp. Point Power: Fairy Lv. 1
	Seafood Pasta	1600	Teensy Power: Grass Lv. 1 Item Drop Power: Rock Lv. 1 Raid Power: Flying Lv. 1
	Four-Piece Sushi (Flower Set)	2000	Catching Power: Steel Lv. 1 Exp. Point Power: Bug Lv. 1 Teensy Power: Dragon Lv. 1
	Four-Piece Sushi (Bird Set)	2000	Teensy Power: Electric Lv. 1 Catching Power: Dragon Lv. 1 Raid Power: Grass Lv. 1
	Four-Piece Sushi (Wind Set)	2000	Item Drop Power: Rock Lv. 1 Teensy Power: Ice Lv. 1 Exp. Point Power: Bug Lv. 1

Meal	Name	Cost	Meal Power
	Four-Piece Sushi (Moon Set)	2000	Exp. Point Power: Fighting Lv. 1 Raid Power: Ground Lv. 1 Egg Power Lv. 1
	Miso Soup	900	Humungo Power: Flying Lv. 1 Item Drop Power: Water Lv. 1 Catching Power: Ice Lv. 1
	Exclusive Four-Piece Sushi (Frost Set)	4000	Raid Power: Water Lv. 2 Egg Power Lv. 1 Item Drop Power: Steel Lv. 1
	Exclusive Four-Piece Sushi (Graupel Set)	4000	Item Drop Power: Dragon Lv. 2 Egg Power Lv. 1 Teensy Power: Electric Lv. 1
	Exclusive Four-Piece Sushi (Hail Set)	4000	Item Drop Power: Dragon Lv. 2 Egg Power Lv. 1 Teensy Power: Electric Lv. 1
	Exclusive Four-Piece Sushi (Sleet Set)	4000	Humungo Power: Steel Lv. 2 Exp. Point Power: Poison Lv. 1 Raid Power: Rock Lv. 1
	Consommé	3500	Catching Power: Ghost Lv. 2 Humungo Power: Water Lv. 1 Encounter Power: Fire Lv. 1
	Mapo Tofu	1700	Encounter Power: Fire Lv. 1 Item Drop Power: Flying Lv. 1 Teensy Power: Psychic Lv. 1
	Annin Tofu	900	Egg Power Lv. 1 Raid Power: Ghost Lv. 1 Teensy Power: Ice Lv. 1

Meal	Name	Cost	Meal Power
	Pickled Toedscool and Cucumber	950	Teensy Power: Ghost Lv. 1 Egg Power Lv. 1 Item Drop Power: Rock Lv. 1
	Pepper Steak	1700	Item Drop Power: Poison Lv. 1 Teensy Power: Grass Lv. 1 Egg Power Lv. 1
	Ramen	1600	Humungo Power: Ground Lv. 1 Catching Power: Normal Lv. 1 Raid Power: Dark Lv. 1
	Galette de la Maman	3000	Humungo Power: Dragon Lv. 2 Catching Power: Electric Lv. 1 Raid Power: Fire Lv. 1
	Compote du Fils	2800	Egg Power Lv. 2 Exp. Point Power: Flying Lv. 1 Encounter Power: Fairy Lv. 1
	Ratatouille du Grand-père	3600	Item Drop Power: Psychic Lv. 2 Encounter Power: Ice Lv. 1 Catching Power: Rock Lv. 1
	Quiche de la Grand-mère	3400	Catching Power: Ice Lv. 2 Exp. Point Power: Fairy Lv. 1 Egg Power Lv. 1
	Pot-au-Feu de la Fille	3800	Teensy Power: Steel Lv. 2 Item Drop Power: Fire Lv. 1 Exp. Point Power: Flying Lv. 1
	Dry Curry	1800	Humungo Power: Fairy Lv. 1 Raid Power: Ground Lv. 1 Catching Power: Water Lv. 1
	Chocolate-Vanilla Fruit Parfait	1400	Catching Power: Ground Lv. 1 Item Drop Power: Dark Lv. 1 Exp. Point Power: Poison Lv. 1

Meal	Name	Cost	Meal Power
	Lemon Gelato	900	Item Drop Power: Ghost Lv. 1 Humungo Power: Rock Lv. 1 Exp. Point Power: Normal Lv. 1
	Caesar Salad	1300	Exp. Point Power: Flying Lv. 1 Teensy Power: Normal Lv. 1 Item Drop Power: Fire Lv. 1
	Salisbury Steak with Fried Fixings	1900	Egg Power Lv. 1 Encounter Power: Flying Lv. 1 Catching Power: Fairy Lv. 1
	Spicy Potatoes	1450	Encounter Power: Dragon Lv. 1 Teensy Power: Dark Lv. 1 Exp. Point Power: Grass Lv. 1
	Alfajores	950	Raid Power: Fighting Lv. 1 Catching Power: Steel Lv. 1 Humungo Power: Dark Lv. 1
	Lemon Soda	900	Teensy Power: Dark Lv. 1 Egg Power Lv. 1 Exp. Point Power: Water Lv. 1
	Coffee	850	Item Drop Power: Water Lv. 1 Exp. Point Power: Grass Lv. 1 Humungo Power: Steel Lv. 1
	Quesadilla	1600	Raid Power: Ghost Lv. 1 Egg Power Lv. 1 Catching Power: Psychic Lv. 1
	Five-Alarm Sandwich	1700	Egg Power Lv. 1 Teensy Power: Steel Lv. 1 Raid Power: Psychic Lv. 1
	Peanut Butter Sandwich	1020	Exp. Point Power: Fairy Lv. 1 Encounter Power: Electric Lv. 1 Teensy Power: Ground Lv. 1

Meal	Name	Cost	Meal Power
	Potato Salad Sandwich	1200	Item Drop Power: Grass Lv. 1 Catching Power: Rock Lv. 1 Teensy Power: Ghost Lv. 1
	Pickle Sandwich	950	Catching Power: Dark Lv. 1 Encounter Power: Rock Lv. 1 Humungo Power: Dragon Lv. 1
	Egg Sandwich	980	Humungo Power: Fighting Lv. 1 Egg Power Lv. 1 Item Drop Power: Poison Lv. 1
	Mustard Rice Ball	750	Encounter Power: Rock Lv. 1 Catching Power: Ice Lv. 1 Humungo Power: Electric Lv. 1
	Sweet Adzuki Bean Soup	800	Exp. Point Power: Normal Lv. 1 Item Drop Power: Steel Lv. 1 Encounter Power: Poison Lv. 1
	Homemade Umeboshi	500	Teensy Power: Fire Lv. 1 Exp. Point Power: Ghost Lv. 1 Egg Power Lv. 1
	Bitter Melon Stir-Fry	950	Item Drop Power: Ground Lv. 1 Humungo Power: Ghost Lv. 1 Encounter Power: Rock Lv. 1
	Soba Noodle Soup	920	Egg Power Lv. 1 Encounter Power: Fire Lv. 1 Raid Power: Grass Lv. 1
	Dandan Noodles	3600	Item Drop Power: Fire Lv. 2 Humungo Power: Grass Lv. 1 Egg Power Lv. 1
	Tofu Pudding	3000	Exp. Point Power: Poison Lv. 2 Encounter Power: Psychic Lv. 1 Raid Power: Ice Lv. 1

Meal	Name	Cost	Meal Power
	Hot and Sour Soup	3200	Egg Power Lv. 2 Item Drop Power: Fairy Lv. 1 Humungo Power: Fighting Lv. 1
	Oolong Tea	2800	Teensy Power: Dragon Lv. 2 Catching Power: Ghost Lv. 1 Item Drop Power: Ice Lv. 1
	House Special Hot Pot	3800	Humungo Power: Rock Lv. 2 Exp. Point Power: Psychic Lv. 1 Catching Power: Steel Lv. 1
	Churro	850	Exp. Point Power: Psychic Lv. 1 Catching Power: Ground Lv. 1 Teensy Power: Fire Lv. 1
	Chocolate Churro	950	Encounter Power: Psychic Lv. 1 Item Drop Power: Bug Lv. 1 Raid Power: Normal Lv. 1
	Cinnamon Churro	900	Catching Power: Dragon Lv. 1 Egg Power Lv. 1 Teensy Power: Grass Lv. 1
	Pinchitos	1200	Item Drop Power: Dark Lv. 1 Teensy Power: Dragon Lv. 1 Exp. Point Power: Rock Lv. 1
	Grilled Rice Balls	950	Encounter Power: Fairy Lv. 1 Teensy Power: Electric Lv. 1 Egg Power Lv. 1
	Strawberry Chocolate Crepe	950	Raid Power: Water Lv. 1 Catching Power: Fairy Lv. 1 Egg Power Lv. 1
	Strawberry Whipped Cream Crepe	950	Exp. Point Power: Ground Lv. 1 Humungo Power: Ice Lv. 1 Encounter Power: Electric Lv. 1

Meal	Name	Cost	Meal Power
	Chocolate Banana Crepe	900	Egg Power Lv. 1 Encounter Power: Water Lv. 1 Teensy Power: Steel Lv. 1
	Mint Chocolate Ice Cream	950	Raid Power: Fairy Lv. 1 Humungo Power: Steel Lv. 1 Egg Power Lv. 1
	Fizzy-Pop Ice Cream	900	Exp. Point Power: Normal Lv. 1 Catching Power: Water Lv. 1 Humungo Power: Fire Lv. 1
	Strawberry Ice Cream	900	Egg Power Lv. 1 Exp. Point Power: Water Lv. 1 Raid Power: Rock Lv. 1
	Mango Ice Cream	900	Teensy Power: Normal Lv. 1 Raid Power: Dragon Lv. 1 Catching Power: Electric Lv. 1
	Nacli Salt Ice Cream	900	Humungo Power: Ice Lv. 1 Item Drop Power: Grass Lv. 1 Catching Power: Dark Lv. 1
	Teriyaki Ice Cream	1150	Item Drop Power: Bug Lv. 1 Raid Power: Fighting Lv. 1 Egg Power Lv. 1

Before you head off into the wild world running around catching Pokémon galore, why not give yourself the edge right from the beginning.

Let's take a look at a few key tips and tricks that'll make your time in the game much more enjoyable and *far* less frustrating…

The Firestarter

If you're looking for the equivalent of "easy mode", then picking *Fuecoco* at the beginning as your starter Pokémon is the way to go.

We consistently found that - across all of the main story-line challenges - our **Fire-type** dominated the vast majority of our opponents. It also evolves naturally via leveling. It's not bullet-proof, but it's a *very* powerful choice as no Pokémon are immune to Fire-type attacks.

Obedience

As S&V is an open-world game, there's nothing stopping you trying to catch a super-high level Pokémon right from the start.

However, even if you manage to defy the - amazingly small - catch odds, the Pokémon *will not* obey your battle commands until you beat enough Gym Trainers.

Beating the first Gym Leader (any), ensures that Pokémon up to Level 20 will obey you. With that level increasing by five for every additional Gym Leader you defeat in battle.

Tera Raids

Tera Raids are awesome as they're relatively easy to beat at the beginning, and they often give you *loads* of cool rewards for defeating the Tera Pokémon inside.

Plus, you're *guaranteed* to catch the Tera Pokémon you just beat - and you can use *any* ball to do it!

Finally, Tera Raids offer you some very nice EXP rewards for the Pokémon that you took in to battle with (such as **Exp. Candy S**, **M**, or **L**). These provide an EXP boost on a Pokémon of your choosing!

Optimal Story-Line Route

While you can go and take on any Gym Leader, Crew, or Titan Pokémon that you want (in any order you like), it's important to note that they have a set Level of Pokémon that you fight.

Therefore, the game has been designed in a way that makes it easier to progress through the story by tackling them in the optimal order.

If you follow this route, then you'll find your progress *far* less frustrating. Naturally, expert Pokémon players can ignore this. But, if you're new to the game and want an easier time of things, then we've got you covered:

Lv.	Challenge	Page No
15	Bug Gym	68
16	Rock Titan	172
17	Grass Gym	72
19	Flying Titan	174
21	Dark Crew	132
24	Electric Gym	78
27	Fire Crew	138
28	Steel Titan	176
30	Water Gym	84
33	Poison Crew	144
36	Normal Gym	90
42	Ghost Gym	94
44	Ground Titan	178
45	Psychic Gym	98
48	Ice Gym	102
51	Fairy Crew	150
55	Dragon Titan	182
56	Fighting Crew	156
60	Elite 4/Champ	106
62	SFS Finale	162
62	PoL Finale	186
62	Rival Battles	120
67	Area Zero	190

Note

SFS = Starfall Street,
PoL = Path of Legends
VR = Victory Road.

CORTONDO GYM DEFEATED!
VICTORY ROAD
OPEN SKY TITAN DEFEATED!
PATH OF LEGENDS

POKÉ MART | Selling
Treasures
Stardust   ₽1,500   × 1
Pearl   ₽1,000   6
Your Total   ₽1,500
Confirm
Stardust
Lovely red sand that flows between the fingers with a loose, silky feel. It can be sold at a low price to shops.
I could give you ₽1,500, if that sounds good?
Ultra Ball   × 1
Star Piece
A small shard of a beautiful gem that gives off a distinctly red sparkle. It can be sold at a high price to shops.
NEW

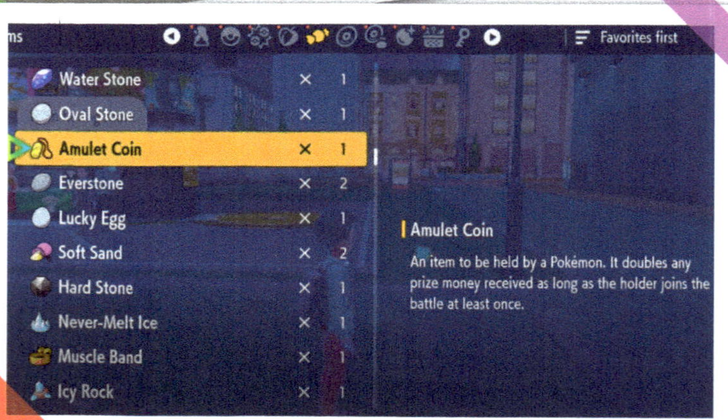
ms   Favorites first
Water Stone   × 1
Oval Stone   × 1
Amulet Coin   × 1
Everstone   × 2
Lucky Egg   × 1
Soft Sand   × 2
Hard Stone   × 1
Never-Melt Ice   × 1
Muscle Band   × 1
Icy Rock   × 1
Amulet Coin
An item to be held by a Pokémon. It doubles any prize money received as long as the holder joins the battle at least once.

You are challenged by Dendra the Instructor!

Quick Money

Here's a few ways in which you can build up that in-game bank balance much quicker than usual…

Sell, sell, sell!

There's a number of different items that you can find on your adventures that Pokémon Centers will gladly buy from you for good money.

Item	Worth
Comet Shards	6000
Damp Rock	2000
Moon Stone	750
Smooth Rock	2000
Soft Sand	750
Stardust	1500
Star Piece	1500

You can often find the items listed above at either the *Asado Desert*, or in *East Province (Area Three)*. Pick up every shiny object from the ground, sell them, save, then reload the area to refresh the random treasure drops.

The Amulet Coin

The Amulet Coin doubles any prize money received as long as the Pokémon holding it joins the battle at least once.

You get it by beating all five of the trainers that are located in *West Province (Area Three)*, then go speak with the Pokémon League rep (located outside the *Medali Pokemon Center*), they'll give you the amulet.

Academy Ace Tournament Farming

Finally, once you unlock the *Academy Ace Tournament* (after beating the main story-line), you can re-take this tournament as often as you like. Pair this up with the **Amulet** for serious cash returns.

This is especially helpful if you're looking to finish off your Pokédex.

Level-Up Quickly

It's possible to take all of your Pokémon up to the lofty heights of Level 100 (essential for those post-game Black Crystal Tera Raids!).

There are a few different ways you can approach this and we'll focus on the non-glitchy ways (in case they get patched out later on):

The "Chansey Method"

Certain Pokemon give you greater amounts of EXP when you defeat them. And, *Chansey* Pokémon provide some of the largest EXP rewards of them all (there *are* others that offer slightly more EXP, but they're *nowhere* near as easy to find in comparison).

You can find Level 40+ *Chansey* Pokémon wandering around the grassy area of *North Province (Area Three)*, close to the *Fairy Crew* base entrance.

Top Tip!

You can take a **Ghost-type** of *any level* to fight them here as they're immune to Chansey's **Normal** attacks!

You can also boost your chances of encounter this **Normal-type** Pokémon even more, by creating a **Ham Sandwich** at a picnic bench, as that activates the Meal Power: **Encounter Power: Normal** to Level 1.

You can purchase all of the ingredients for the recipe from the *Aquiesta Supermarket in Levincia*. Buy enough for a few sandwiches.

Once you're ready, head back to the *North Province (Area Three)* quick travel area, set up a picnic, make your sandwich and then **save your game manually**.

Now just walk down the hill and it's you'll - more-than-likely - encounter **loads** of *Chanseys* walking around!

Fight them until your **Meal Power** wears off, then go back up, eat a new sandwich, rinse and repeat as required!

After beating five Gym Leaders, go speak with Mr. Jacq in Biology class for a **Lucky Egg** that *doubles* the amount of EXP that the Pokémon holding receives (so, give it to your best Pokémon!)

Combine that with Chansey battles to **seriously** boost the amount of EXP that you earn per battle!

As their levels increase, so too will the amount of EXP you earn. As a side-benefit, once you've beaten all key Trainers in a set area, speak with the *Pokémon League Rep* for a freebie for your efforts!

Grab the Poké Balls

Laying on the ground across the whole world are Red and Yellow Poké Balls. These balls always provide you with free items that you can use in your adventure. The items within the Red Balls are random, while the Yellow Balls give you a TM of some description. Be sure to collect all of them on your adventure!

Defeating other Trainers

In each area, you'll soon begin to notice lots of people standing around on their own. These people are Trainers (if their speech bubble is highlighted in yellow). Approach one to initiate a battle with them.

Evolutions
Bigger, faster, stronger

One of the key features in the Pokémon series is the ability for your Pokémon to evolve over time.

Every time they evolve (usually each Pokémon can evolve 2 - 3 times), they become stronger and they often take on additional Types (making them "Dual-types").

Dual-types have a wider-range of move types to draw upon.

There's a few different ways Pokémon can evolve in S&V (with some of them being *anything* but obvious), so we'll take a brief look at each of them:

Leveling Up

The vast majority of Pokémon evolve as soon as you hit the level required to do so.

Use Candy's found around the world (or in Tera Raids) to accelerate this process.

Get those steps in!

A few Pokémon require you to make them walk 1,000 steps in "Let's Go!" and have them auto-battle it out until they get the 1,000 steps in (and then the next time they level-up, they'll evolve).

Notable 1,000 step evolutions examples include:

- *Pawmo into Pawmot*
- *Bramblin into Brambleghast*
- *Rellor into Rabsca*

Time-of-day Evolutions

A few Pokémon require their evolutions to occur at a specific time of the day. Notable examples include:

- *Rockruff into Lycanroc (Dusk Form) at Sunset.*
- *Greavard into Houndstone at Night.*

Evolution Items

You can find a number of different items and stones that can be used on specific Pokémon to trigger their evolution (once they level-up while holding it).

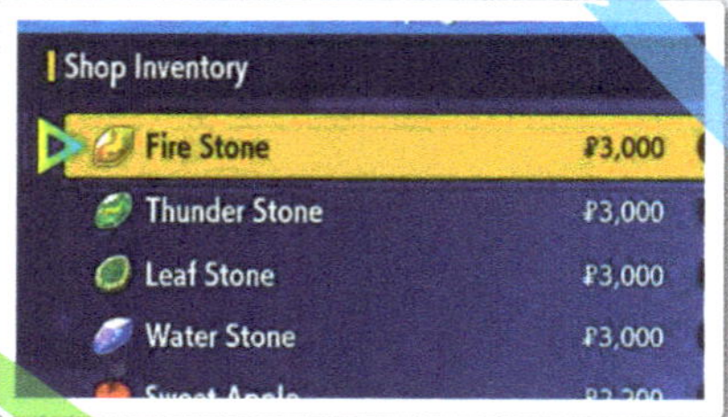

Such stones include the **Thunder Stone**, **Fire Stone**, **Moon Stone**, **Leaf Stone,** and more.

A full list of evolution items (and which Pokémon they evolve), can be found starting at *page 279.*

Side-quests

Some Pokémon require you to complete a series of steps and then trade some specific items to someone in return for the evolution item.

A perfect example is *Charcadet* who requires you to collect 10 x **Bronzor Fragments** (only available in Scarlet) which you must then

give to a man standing around in the town of *Zapapico.*

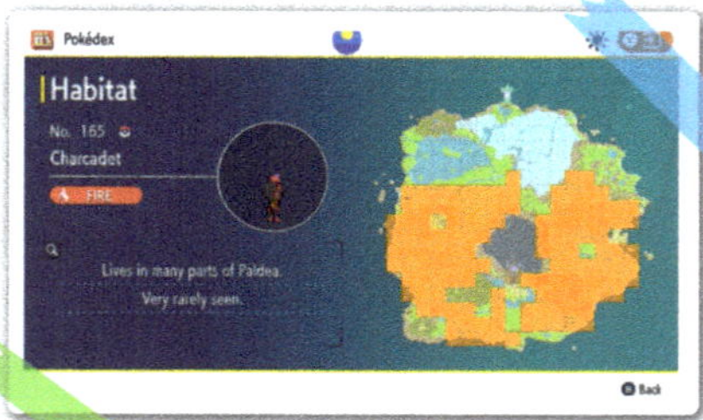

Or, you can catch a *Sinistea* in Violet and then collect 10x **Sinistea Chips** and then trade those items with the same person in *Zapapico.*

Co-op Evolution

If you've managed to catch a *Finizen* already, then you'll need to get it up to Lv. 38 *while playing in co-op mode* (either online with strangers, or with a friend).

If your *Finizen* is above this level when you do it, no problem, just give it some Candy to level-up one more time (while in co-op mode) to evolve it into a *Palafin*!

Switch your *Palafin* out during a battle and *bring it back in again* to see it has changed into its **Hero form**! This new form boasts a boost to most of its stats (and a whole new look!).

Egg Breeding

Another method some Pokémon require you to use is to breed them so they create eggs that - hopefully - hatch into a rarer breed/evolution.

One example is the three-segmented *Dundunsparce* that *can* be caught in the wild (but is a very low percentage chance).

If you get two *Dunsparces* to breed (using the TM **Hyper Drill**), then they'll produce eggs with a much higher chance of becoming the rarer three-segmented version of *Dundunsparce*.

High Friendship Level

A Pokémon such as *Riolu* requires that your friendship level is high-enough. You can check the current level of your friendship with any Pokémon by speaking with the NPC character located in *Cascarrafa*.

You can also give a **Soothe Bell** to the Pokémon to quickly speed this process up.

One *Riolu's* friendship level is high-enough, it evolves into *Lucario* at its next level-up.

Gimmi those 999+ coins!

If you've spotted those chests around the game (especially those at the top of every watchtower), then you can capture the *Gimmighoul* inside.

Once caught, collect a whopping **999+** of the **Gimmighoul Coins** that they drop! Level-up to see it transform into a *Gholdengo*!

Class Act
How to pass those exams

One commonly overlooked area of the game are the Academy Classes that you can take. They're not required for finishing the story-line, but they do offer you further insights into the world and the teachers often give you rewards for completing their side-quests.

To start the classes, you must speak with the receptionist at the front desk of the Academy and tell her which class you want to take. Here are the rewards on offer for completing each class:

Teacher	Reward
Dendra	10 X Protein
Director Clavell	Big Nugget
Hassel	50x **Dragon** Tera Shards
Jacq	TM057: **False Swipe**
Raifort	TM 140: **Nasty Plot**
Saguaro	Herba Mystica Quest
Salvatore	Galarian Meowth
Tyme	50x **Rock** Tera Shards

However, there *are* exams that you need to also pass in order to claim those sweet, sweet rewards. Thankfully, that's where this guide comes in to make those exams easy.

Let's break the classes down into their subjects and then into their individual exams:

Art Class (Lessons)

Lesson	Answer
1	No correct answer.
2	The **Grass-type**.
3	The **Ice-type**.
4	No correct answer.
5	Glaseado's Grasp.
6	Change their title

Art Class (Mid-term)

Question	Answer
What is the name of the gemstone that glows over a Pokémon's head when it Terastallizes?	Tera Jewel.
When the answer to question 1 is in the shape of flowers, what type does it represent?	The Grass type.
What shape are most snowflakes classified as?	Hexagon
Where is the eatery that allows you to change a Tera Type?	Medali.
What makes something beautiful?	No correct answer.

Art Class (Final Exam)

Question	Answer
What is the name of the restaurant where you can change a Pokémon's Tera Type?	The Treasure Eatery.
What is the name of Brassius's signature art installation that we discussed in class?	Surrendering Sunflora.
How many waterfalls are counted among the Ten Sights of Paldea?	Two.
Where can you find the Million Volt Skyline?	Levincia.
The marks a Pokémon has are present when you first meet and none can be added later.	False.

Battle Class (Lessons)

Lesson	Answer
1	Physical moves and special moves.
2	Heal up!
3	Terastallize and attack it.
4	N/A
5	LP
6	Flat Rules.

Battle Class (Mid-term)

Question	Answer
The higher a Pokémon's Sp. Def, the less damage it takes from ____ attacks.	Special.
Which of the following has no effect on a move's damage?	The move's name.
How many Trainers are on a Tera Raid Battle team?	Four.
What is an effective method for breaking an opponent's Tera Shield?	Terastallizing and attacking.
What is Ms. Dendra's favorite type?	Fighting.

Battle Class (Finals)

Question	Answer
Which cheer boosts Attack and Sp. Atk for all allies during a Tera Raid Battle?	*Go all out!*
What do we call the battles that Pokémon sent out with the R Button do on their own?	*Auto Battles.*
How should you obtain LP?	*Exchange materials.*
High-level Pokémon are adjusted to what level when using Flat Rules in Link Battles?	*Lv. 50*
When using Normal Rules in Link Battles, you can use multiple Pokémon of the same species and multiples of the same held item.	*True.*

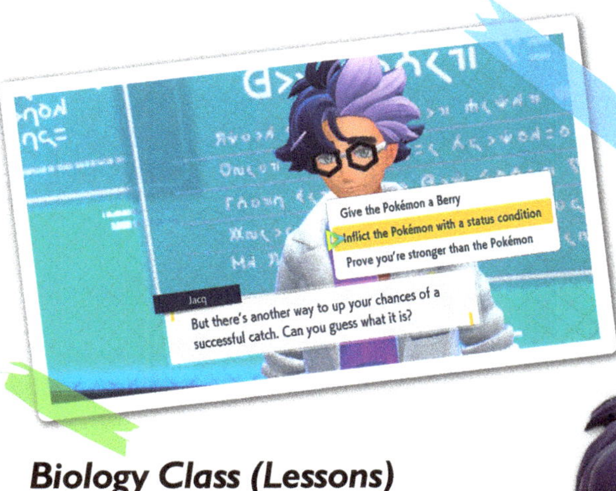

Biology Class (Lessons)

Lesson	Answer
1	*Inside buildings.*
2	*Eggs!*
3	*Inflict the Pokémon with a status condition.*
4	*B Button!*
5	*1 in 4,000*
6	*Change their title.*

Biology Class (Mid-term)

Question	Answer
What button would you use to let a Pokémon out of its ball so that it can walk with you?	ZR button.
Combine one letter and one number below to correctly say when and where Eggs are found.	A2 - During picnics in your basket.
Which of the following is an effective way to warm up Eggs?	Walking around.
What will NOT make Pokémon easier to catch?	Giving them a Berry.
What will make it easier to catch Pokémon of higher and higher levels?	Gym badges.

Biology Class (Finals)

Question	Answer
How many of the following four methods make it easier to catch a Pokémon?…	Two.
True or false? You can get new Pokémon only by catching them yourself or trading with other trainers.	False.
If a Pokémon is holding an Everstone, will using an item that induces Evolution, such as a Fire Stone, cause it to evolve?	Two.
What is the probability of running into a Shiny Pokémon?	No, it won't.
True or false? The Pokémon known as Oricorio has three forms.	False.

Home Ec (Lessons)

Lesson	Answer
1	My choice of fillings and condiments.
2	Items on the ground.
3	It can't use moves.
4	He should make food with other people.
5	Clean it up.
6	Our Rotom phones?

Home Ec Class (Mid-term)

Question	Answer
Which is not an effect of a picnic meal?	Increasing Speed.
Which of the following affects the kinds of Meal Powers received from a particular meal?	Fillings and condiments.
Which of these Berries can restore a Pokémon's HP?	Oran Berry.
Leandro wanted his Pokémon to decide on its own when to use its item in battle, so he gave it an Oran Berry. This will work as he hopes.	True.
If a move runs out of PP, it can no longer be used. If a Pokémon runs out of PP for all its moves, it can only sit there in frustration.	False.

Home Ec Class (Finals)

Question	Answer
How many of the following four methods make it easier to catch a Pokémon?…	*Two.*
True or false? You can get new Pokémon only by catching them yourself or trading with other trainers.	*False.*
If a Pokémon is holding an Everstone, will using an item that induces Evolution, such as a Fire Stone, cause it to evolve?	*Two.*
What is the probability of running into a Shiny Pokémon?	*No, it won't.*
True or false? The Pokémon known as *Oricorio* has three forms.	False.

History (Lessons)

Lesson	Answer
1	*Treasure.*
2	*About two thousand years ago.*
3	*About eight hundred years ago.*
4	*Wooden plans for writing on.*
5	*The Area Zero Expedition.*
6	*Professor Sada (Scarlet) or, Professor Turo (Violet).*

History Class (Mid-term)

Question	Answer
What is the name of the geological formation in the center of the Paldea region?	*The Great Crater of Paldea.*
What was long believed to rest in the depths of Area Zero?	*Treasure.*
How many years ago did the Paldea Empire begin to rule this region?	*Approximately 2,000 years ago.*
How many years ago was this academy built?	*805 years ago.*
Those seeking _______ need look no further than the oranges / grapes of Paldea.	*Knowledge.*

History Class (Finals)

Question	Answer
What is the area within the Great Crater of Paldea called?	*Area Zero.*
How many years ago was the academy founded?	*805 years ago.*
Which of these did not appear in the Paldea fairy tale about the four treasures?	*A folding fan.*
Which Area Zero Expedition member wrote the record of the team's activities?	*Heath.*
How many years ago did Professor Sada / Turo invent Tera Orbs?	*10 years ago.*

Language (Lessons)

Lesson	Answer
1	*Thank you.*
2	*Delicious.*
3	*I love you.*
4	*Anger.*
5	*Sadness.*
6	*Happiness.*

Language Class (Mid-term)

Question	Answer
Gracias, arigato, merci, and xièxie all share the same meaning. What is it?	Thank you.
Which of the following means delicious?	Délicieux.
Which of these phrases doesn't belong?	Time to eat.
When speaking with a person, what is the first step to smooth communication?	Compliment them.
What is your beloved teacher's name?	Salvatore.

Language Class (Finals)

Question	Answer
Which of the following means delicious?	Délicieux.
What do these two foreign phrases mean? Je t'aime! Ich liebe dich!	I love you.
Based on what you just heard, what emotion do you think Pikachu was expressing?	Anger.
Based on what you just heard, what emotion do you think Pikachu was expressing?	Happiness.
What is your beloved teacher's name?	Salvatore.

Maths Class (Lessons)

Lesson	Answer
1	It's doubled.
2	11
3	About 4% (4 in 100 hits).
4	Triple damage.
5	Any answer.
6	Its power becomes 300.

Maths Class (Mid-term)

Question	Answer
How much damage does Water Gun do when it hits a Fire-type Pokémon?	Double damage.
How much damage does Razor Leaf do when it hits a Fire-type Pokémon?	Half damage.
If you spent 2,000 Pokécoins on as many 200 Pokécoin Poké Balls as possible, how many would you get	Eleven
What percentage chance does a Pokémon usually have to land a critical hit?	About 4%
How much damage does a move deal when it lands a critical hit?	One-and-a-half times as much..

Maths Class (Finals)

Question	Answer
How many Great Balls could you purchase with 3,000 Pokécoins if each one costs 600?	Five.
If a Water-type move with a power of 200 lands a critical hit on a Grass-type Pokémon, what will the move's power be?	75
Under normal conditions, what percent chance does Stone Edge have to land a critical hit?	About 12 percent.
If a Pokémon uses Swords Dance twice to boost its Attack by four stages, how much damage will its physical moves then do?	Triple Damage.
If a Rock-type Pokemon whose Tera Type is Rock Terastallizes, what will the power of its Rock-type moves be multiplied by?	2

Gym Leader Brassius sent out Petilil!

Victory Road
Classic Gym Battles

Even though S&V is an open-world Pokémon game, the classical gym battles are back.

The Victory Road path is one of the three main quests you can pursue (although, you *can* take them on in *any* order this time).

We're going to make this easier for you by giving you all the info you need upfront, so *you* can decide which order to go for.

However, we *will* list them in the order that takes you from easiest to hardest. Whether you take them on in that order? Well, that's entirely up to you.

However, bear in mind that the Gyms **do not** scale up to your current level. They're all fixed, meaning you can find yourself going in at a *far* lower level than required…

Note

In order to get access to the Gym's leaders, you'll first need to pass the associated "Gym Test." Each test is made up of a mini-game of sorts, along with battles against lower-level Gym trainers.

Of course, don't worry, as we've got the solutions to each test already all mapped out for you. You've got this!

Tera (Fire)
Tera (Rock)

Bug Gym
Route & Gym Test

Your Goals:

- *Level up Pokémon team to Lv. 15,*
- *Locate the Bug Gym,*
- *Pass the Gym Test,*
- *Fight the Gym Leader.*

1: Build your team

Thanks to the benefit of our hindsight, we'll tell you which Pokémon are worth catching, and leveling up, *before* you get anywhere close to the Gym.

Bug-types are weak to: **Fire, Flying,** and **Rock-types.**

Picked **Fuecoco** as your starter? Then leveling it up will prove *very* useful.

Otherwise, catch and train up the following:

- *Diglett (Rock Tera-type),*
- *Fletchling (Normal/Flying),*
- *Starly (Normal/Flying).*

Spend some time using auto-battle now to get your whole team up to Lv. 15.

2: Bug Gym Location

The Bug Gym is located in *Cortondo.* Set this location as a way-point on your mini-map to make it easier to find.

3. Pass the Gym Test

This test, known as the *Olive Roll Challenge,* can be located north of the Pokémon Center on the map.

Push the giant, bouncy, olive around the maze. Save time by knocking the olive *over* the barriers! Very sneaky!

Gym Battle:
Vs. Gym Leader Kathy

Pokémon	Level	Type	Weakness
	14		
	14		
	15		

As this is the first gym battle in the game, it won't be very difficult at all (assuming you followed our tips on the previous page and caught and leveled up the correct Pokémon).

Nymble should go down very quickly and its moves won't pose much of a threat.

Tarountula shouldn't pose much of a threat either as it is identical in level to *Nymble*.

All Gym leaders will **Terrastallize** their final Pokémon. In this case, turning it into a Bug-type.

Teddiusra is a **Normal-type** Pokémon that changes into a **Bug-type**.

Rewards:

* *2,700 money*
* *TM021* **Pounce**
* *Ability to catch Lv. 25+ Pokémon.*

Nymble
Crocalor used Ember!
Teddiursa
CORTONDO GYM DEFEATED!
VICTORY ROAD

Grass Gym
Route & Gym Test

Your Goals:

- *Level up Pokémon team to Lv. 17,*
- *Locate the Grass Gym,*
- *Pass the Gym Test,*
- *Fight the Gym Leader.*

1: Build your team

Picked **Fuecoco** as your starter? Then leveling it up to Lv. 18 will prove very useful.

Otherwise, catch and train up the following:

- *Charcadet (Fire),*
- *Litleo (Fire/Normal),*
- *Rookidee (Flying).*

Spend some time using auto-battle now to get your whole team up to Lv. 17.

2: Grass Gym Location

Located in *Artazon* (located east of *Mesagoza*).

Set this location as a way-point on your mini-map to make it easier to find.

3. Pass the Gym Test

This test, known as the *Hide-and-Seek Challenge*, can be located just outside the gym entrance.

The goal is to locate 10 hidden **Sunfloras**.

1 - 3. Located behind you.

4. By a street light, left of Gym (you must fight it first).

5. At the small pond by the maze.

6. The end of the pond's walkway.

7. Middle of stone artwork.

8. In between park benches.

9. Northeast of Pokémon Center.

10. Under kid's play area, near the swimming pool.

1 - 3
Collected?

4
Lv. 13
Sunflora
Tackle
Incinerate
Ember
Round
Lv. 23
Crocalor
TERASTALLIZE!
Move Info
Collected?

6
5
Collected?
Collected?

7
Collected?
Collected?
9
8
Collected?
Collected?
10

Gym Battle:
Vs. Gym Leader Brassius

Pokémon	Level	Type	Weakness
	16	Grass	Fire, Flying, Ice, Poison, Bug
	16	Grass	Fire, Flying, Ice, Poison, Bug
	17	Rock / Grass	Fighting, Ground, Steel, Water, Grass, Fire, Flying, Ice, Poison, Bug

As **Grass-types** are weak to the same types as **Bug-types** are, your team should be ready to go (assuming you're following the same order).

Petilil can put you to sleep (**Sleep Powder**) or steal your HP (**Mega Drain**). Use your strongest Pokémon first.

Smoliv is much easier to handle (compared to *Petilil*) if you use a super-effective move on it.

Sudowoodo is a cool **Rock-type** Pokémon that TT's into a **Grass-type**.

Use your fastest Pokémon on it as it can up its own speed. Will take a few hits to remove.

Rewards:

- *3,060 money*
- *TM020 **Trailblaze***
- *Ability to catch Lv. 30+ Pokémon.*

Gym Leader Brassius sent out Petilil!
Smoliv
Crocalor used Ember!
Sudowoodo
Crocalor used Ember!
ARTAZON GYM DEFEATED!
VICTORY ROAD

Electric Gym
Route & Gym Test

Your Goals:

- *Level up Pokémon team to Lv. 25,*
- *Locate the Electric Gym,*
- *Pass the Gym Test,*
- *Fight the Gym Leader.*

1: Build your team

Electric-types are weak to **Ground-types** (*except* for Wattrel, which is immune). Therefore, make sure you've got 1 - 2 leveled up and leading your team in this battle.

Otherwise, catch and train up the following:

- • Diglett (Ground),
- • Silicobra (Ground),
- • Rolycoly (Rock).

Spend some time using auto-battle now to get your whole team up to Lv. 25.

2: Electric Gym Location

The Electric Gym is located in *Levincia*.

Caution

To reach this Gym, you can either beat *Team Star's Fire Crew*, a *Titan* (*Bombidier*), or jump across the river to the lowered bank (eastern side of the map).

3. Pass the Gym Test

It's time to play some Hide-and-Seek With "Mr. Walksabout"! Note, that each time after finding him, you'll need to do battle with a trainer.

Top Tip!

Be sure to switch to your Ground-types *now*, as you'll need them for the smaller battles coming up…

You can find him sitting under the parasol, on the right-side of the screen. Nice and easy…

Trainer Battle: Marti

Prize: 3,080

Pokémon	Level	Type	Weakness
	22		

He's now trying that *little bit harder* to hide from you.

This time, you'll find him standing inside the Pokémon Center.

Time for the last Trainer battle before the Gym Leader. This time, you're up against *two* Electric-types.

Pokémon	Level	Type	Weakness
	22	⚡	
	22	⚡	

Trainer Battle: Michael

Prize: 3,080

He's now *really* trying to blend in with the crowd!

Look to the far-right of the screen, and you should *just about* spot him standing there on a back of a boat.

Just off the right-side of the battle arena. Highlight him and Voila! Gym Test passed!

There's no more Trainers to defeat, so you're welcome to heal up your Pokémon and then take them right back into battle.

Let's go for the next badge!

Pokémon	Level	Type	Weakness
	23	⚡ / 🪶	❄ / ◯
	23	⚡	⛰
	23	⚡	⛰
	24	👻 / ⚡	👻 / 🌑 / ⛰

Bring our your *Rolycoly* to the first battle against *Wattrel* as it's weak against Rock-types.

However, it's *Bellibolt* that you need to be wary of. He can use **Water Gun** (which is super effective against Ground-types! How rude!). Use speed items to help give you the edge and Terastallize if it's available.

Luxio can paralyze you, but it's not as sneaky as *Bellibolt*, so use your Ground moves on it.

Finally, *TT-Mismagius* is a cool **Ghost-type** Pokémon that TT's into an **Electric-type**.

This means it *can* still use **Confuse Ray**, so keep **Ghost** or **Psychic** types out of this fight!

Be sure to heal when your Pokémon are starting to feel tired.

Rewards:

- 4,320 money
- TM048 **Volt Switch**
- *Ability to catch Lv. 35+ Pokémon.*

Water Gym
Route & Gym Test

Your Goals:

- *Level up Pokémon team to Lv. 30,*
- *Locate the Water Gym,*
- *Pass the Gym Test,*
- *Fight the Gym Leader.*

1: Build your team

Water-types are weak to both **Grass** and **Electric-types**, but are super strong against **Rock, Ground,** and **Fire-types**.

Which means it's time to make sure we pick (and level-up) the best Pokémon for the job!

We recommend the following:

- *Pawmo (Electric),*
- *Kilowattrel (Flying/Electric),*
- *Skiploom (Grass/Flying).*

Spend some time using auto-battle now to get your whole team up to Lv. 30.

2: Water Gym Location

The Water Gym is located in *Cascarrafa* (which is on the opposite side of the map from the last Gym).

If you see the *Team Star Dark Crew's Base*, move around it and continue north.

3. Pass the Gym Test

The goal is to reach *Port Marinada* via the nearby *Asado Desert* and give **Kofu** back his wallet.

Leave *Cascarrafa* via the northern exit, then go north-west until you reach the exit.

Continue following **Kofu** until you encounter Trainer Hugo. Take out his two **Water** Pokémon and then try and win his **Seaweed** at the auction.

If you can get it for less than 50,000, you'll keep the difference! Sweet!

Pokémon	Level	Type	Weakness
(Veluza)	29	Water / Psychic	Grass, Electric, Bug, Ghost, Dark
(Wugtrio)	29	Water	Grass, Electric
(Crabominable)	30	Fighting / Ice / Water	Fire, Fighting, Flying, Fairy, Steel, Grass, Electric

Keep your **Grass-type** away from the first fight, as *Veluza* can use **Pluck**! An **Electric-type** will work wonders here.

Feel free to switch to a **Grass-type** against *Wugtrio*. It'll be weak against you and it doesn't have any really strong attacks. Onwards.

Finally, *TT-Crabominable* is a cool **Fighting/Ice-type** Pokémon that TT's into a **Water-type**.

Use speed-enhancements to try and get attacks in first, as its **Chilling Water** move can sap your power and lower your attack stat!

Use your fastest Pokémon that is on its weak list to win!

Rewards:

- 5,400 money
- TM022 **Chilling Water**
- Ability to catch Lv. 40+ Pokémon.

Pikachu used Thunderbolt!

The opposing Crabominable fainted!

CASCARRAFA GYM DEFEATED!
VICTORY ROAD

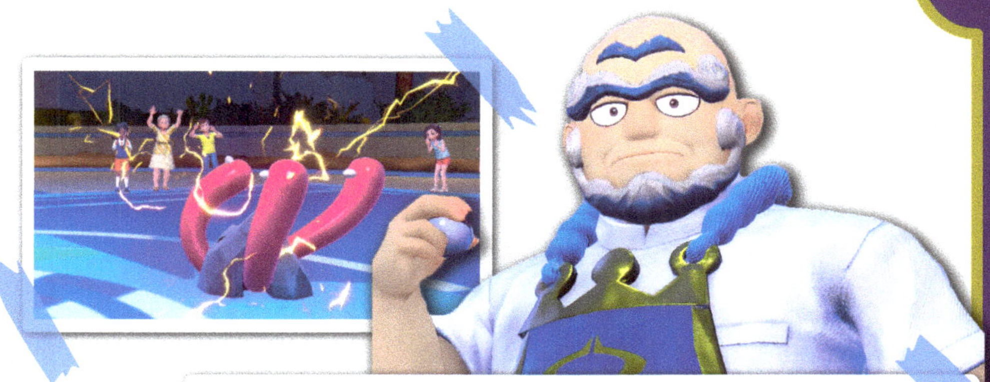

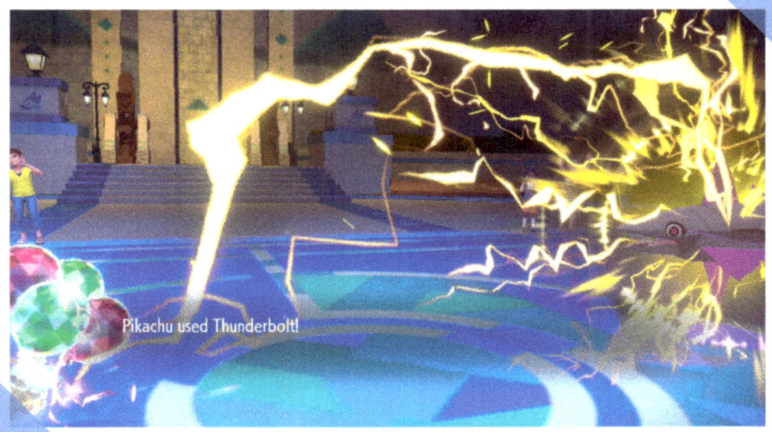

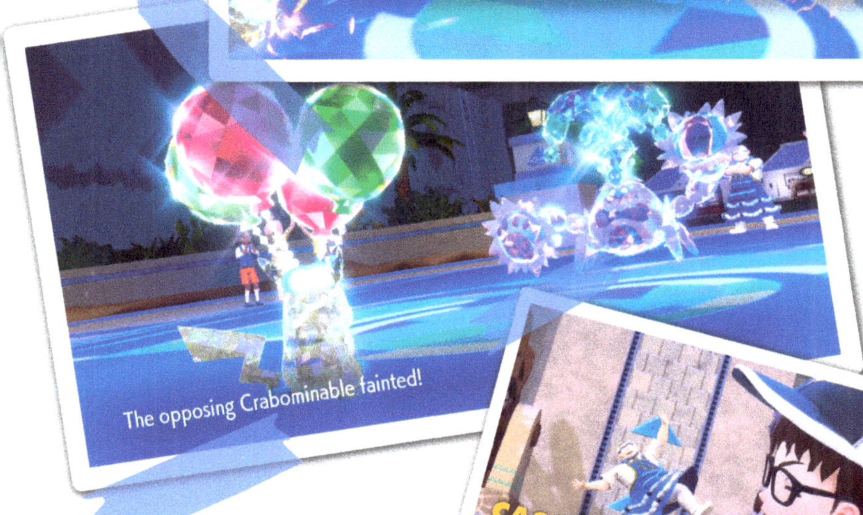

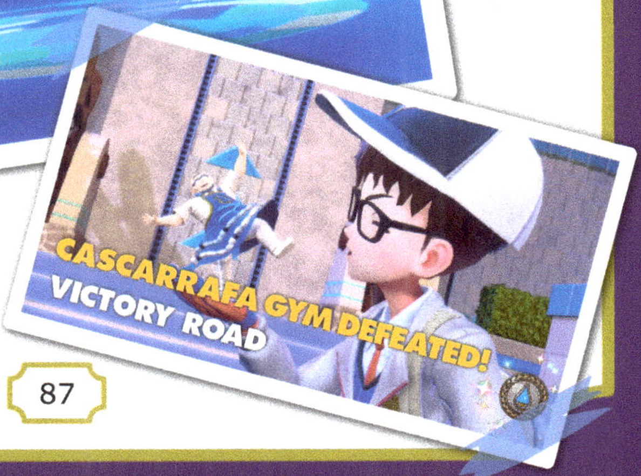

Normal Gym
Route & Gym Test

Your Goals:

- *Level up Pokémon team to Lv. 36,*
- *Locate the Normal Gym,*
- *Pass the Gym Test,*
- *Fight the Gym Leader.*

1: Build your team

Most **Normal-types** are *only* weak to **Fighting-types**. However, **Ghost-types** are also immune to Normal-type moves, so try and catch a *Gengar* and teach it some Fighting moves (it makes the final Gym battle *much* easier!).

Which means it's time to make sure we pick (and level-up) the best Pokémon for the job!

We recommend the following:

- *Pawmo (Electric/Fighting),*
- *Gengar (Ghost/Poison).*

Spend some time using auto-battle now to get your whole team up to Lv. 36.

2: Normal Gym Location

The Normal Gym is located in *Medali* (which is located northeast from *Cascarrafa*).

3. Pass the Gym Test

The goal is to *Order the secret menu item.* While you *could* guess the ingredients required, we've obviously got the solution for you.

However, inputting the order *without obtaining the clues first* means that you'll miss out on several Trainer battles (meaning less EXP and less money).

Skip to the very end of the next page (bypassing each Trainer battle info in the process) for the solution.

For the first clue, speak to the *Office Worker* at the end of the bar.

Head outside, then speak to the student outside the *Treasury Eatery* (with the **golden speech bubble**). Beat her in battle to earn her clue.

Trainer Battle: Adara

Pokémon	Level	Type	Weakness
	34	◎	✊
	34	◎	✊

With Adara's clue now in the bag, it's time to find clue number two.

Head down one of the side-alleys and look for the guy with the golden speech bubble (asking if anyone is "taking the Gym Test?").

He's your next battle! Get to it!

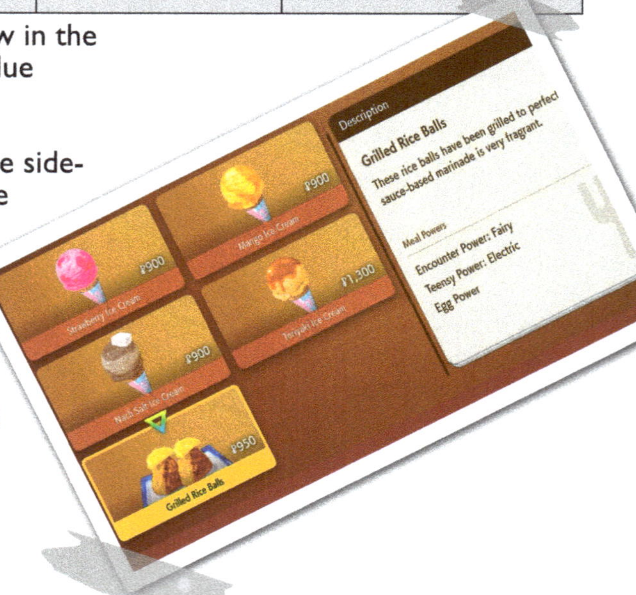

Trainer Battle: Santiago

Pokémon	Level	Type	Weakness
	34	◎	✊

Once you've defeated this one Pokémon, and obtained another clue, it's time to find the next Trainer to fight for their prized tidbit of information.

Make your way to the local Pokémon Center and you'll find *Gisela* standing by a nearby tree. Time to battle!

Trainer Battle: Gisela

Secret Menu Recipe

Pokémon	Level	Type	Weakness
	34	◎	✊

After the battle, head down the semi-circle set of steps to your east and stand by the gate.

Ask for:

"Medium-serving grilled rice balls, Fire Blast style, with fresh lemon on the side!"

Pokémon	Level	Type	Weakness
	35	⬜	✊
	35	⬜	✊
	36	⬜ 🪶 ⬜	✊ ⬜ ⚡ ❄ ✊

Bring out your strongest Pokémon and hit *Komala* hard and fast! Otherwise, it'll send you to sleep, leaving you wide open to its Slam attack!

Dudunsparce can paralyze you and hit you hard with **Hyper Drill**.

Finally, *TT-Staraptor* will intimidate your Pokémon as soon as the battle starts!

We **strongly** recommend that you not only use *Gengar* (or similar), but that you switch out **immediately** if hit with a status move! *Facade* causes **double damage** when you're burned, paralyzed, or poisoned! Ouch!

Also, be careful of its *Aerial Ace* move. It **always** hits you!

Rewards:

- 6,480 money
- TM025 **Facade**
- Ability to catch Lv. 45+ Pokémon.

Komala's
Comatose
MEDALI GYM DEFEATED!
VICTORY ROAD

Your Goals:

- *Level up Pokémon team to Lv. 42,*
- *Locate the Ghost Gym,*
- *Pass the Gym Test,*
- *Fight the Gym Leader.*

1: Build your team

Most **Ghost-types** are only weak to **Dark**, and (ironically) other **Ghost-types**! Also note that they're immune to **Normal** and **Fighting**-based moves. Sneaky. Be sure to catch a *Sableye* as it's both effective types in one!

Ghost vs **Ghost = (2x the damage).** No risk, no reward!

We recommend the following:

- *Tinkatuff (Fairy/Steel),*
- *Sableye (Dark/Ghost),*
- *Gengar (Ghost/Poison).*

Now get your whole team up to Lv. 42 for this Gym.

2: Ghost Gym Location

The Ghost Gym is located in *Montenevera* (which is located near the *Glaseasdo Mountain*).

3. Pass the Gym Test

Beat all three 2v2 Trainer battles to win!

Gym Trainer: Tas

Pokémon	Weakness
Greavard	Dark, Ghost
Shuppet	Dark, Ghost

Gym Trainer: Lani

Pokémon	Weakness
Haunter	Dark, Ghost
Misdreavus	Dark, Ghost, Ground, Fairy

Gym Trainer: MC Sledge

Pokémon	Weakness
Drifblim	Dark, Ghost, Ice, Electric
Sableye	Fairy

Gym Battle:
Vs. Gym Leader Ryme

Pokémon	Level	Type	Weakness
Mimikyu + Banette	41	Ghost	Ghost + Dark
Houndstone	41	Ghost	Ghost
Toxtricity	36	Electric / Poison / Ghost	Ground / Psychic / Ghost

Know that each win (on either side) results in a status boost from the crowd! And focus on only one enemy at a time!

Mimikyu requires two hits due to **Disguise**. Use *Tinkaton* for this fight.

Hit *Banette* hard and fast with your strongest and fastest **Ghost/Dark** type Pokémon.

Use your quickest Pokémon to counter *Houndstone's* **Phantom Force** move. Otherwise, you can't hit it!

Finally, use your overall fastest and strongest Pokémon and Terastallize against *Toxtricity*. Its status moves hit hard and fast, so use your battle items if required.

Rewards:

- 7,800 money
- TM041 **Shadow Ball**
- Ability to catch Lv. 50+ Pokémon.

143
MONTENEVERA GYM DEFEATED!
VICTORY ROAD

Psychic Gym
Route & Gym Test

Your Goals:

- *Level up Pokémon team to Lv. 45,*
- *Locate the Psychic Gym,*
- *Pass the Gym Test,*
- *Fight the Gym Leader.*

1: Build your team

Due to the upcoming mix-and-match of **Psychic** and **Fairy-types,** try and stick with a solid **Bug/ Ghost/Steel-type** team.

Dark-types are great *until* the leader's last Pokémon (which is where a leveled-up *Tinkaton* comes in).

We recommend the following:

- *Lokix (Bug/Dark),*
- *Sableye (Dark/Ghost),*
- *Tinkatuff (Fairy/Steel).*

Now get your whole team up to Lv. 45 for this Gym.

2: Psychic Gym Location

The Psychic Gym is located in *Alfornada* (which requires you to learn how to jump high - which means beating a Titan Pokémon *before* you can attempt this gym).

Jump to page 178 to learn how to beat the *Lurking Steel Titan* Pokémon.

3. Pass the Gym Test

This test is… somewhat *different.* You need to press the button that corresponds to the correct emotion four times.

However, you'll also battle a different Trainer in-between busting out your emotional "dance moves."

Gym Battle:
Vs. Gym Leader Tulip

Pokémon	Level	Type	Weakness
	44		
	44		
	44		
	45		

Lead with *Lokix* when fighting *Farigiraf*, as it's completely weak to it.

For *Gardevoir*, use some Speed boosts on your *Sableye* (or *Tinkaton*) and use your strongest **Ghost** or **Steel** moves.

Hit *Espathra* with a fully-powered up *Lokix*. Boost its Att stat to end this battle ASAP.

Finally, bring out *Tinkaton* give it some auto-heal items, boost your Speed stat, and go toe-to-toe against *Florges*. Stay strong!

Rewards:

- 8,100 *money*
- TM120 **Psychic**
- *Ability to catch Lv. 55+ Pokémon.*

The opposing Espathra used Psychic!
ALFORNADA GYM DEFEATED!
VICTORY ROAD

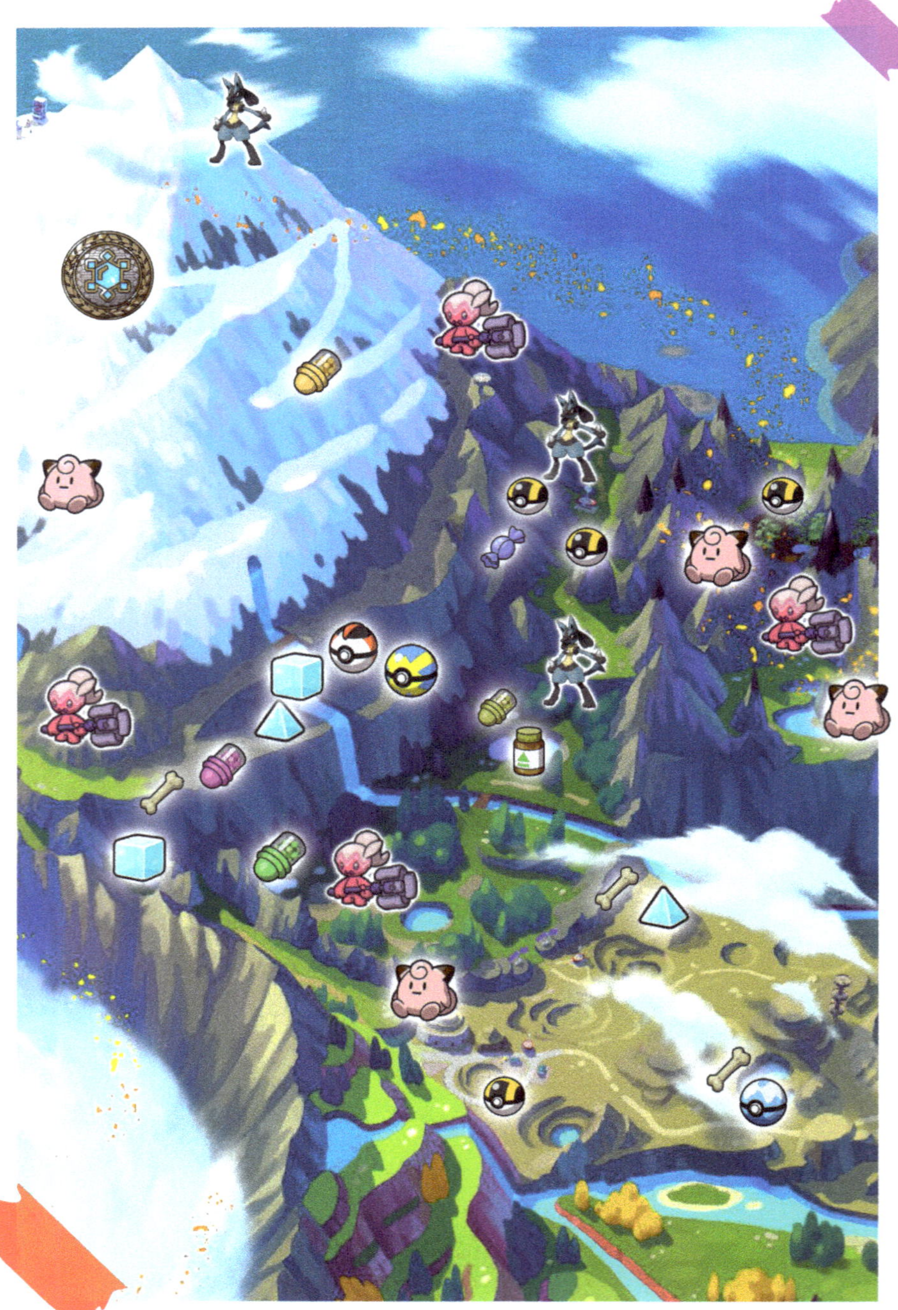

Ice Gym
Route & Gym Test

Your Goals:

- Level up Pokémon team to Lv. 48,
- Locate the Ice Gym,
- Pass the Gym Test,
- Fight the Gym Leader.

1: Build your team

Ice types are, naturally, weak against Fire. (handy for those who picked Fuecoco as their starter).

They're also weak to Steel, Rock, and Fighting-types.

We recommend the following:

- *Skeledirge (Fire/Ghost),*
- *Lucario (Fighting/Steel),*
- *Tinkatuff (Fairy/Steel).*

Now get your whole team up to Lv. 48 for this Gym.

2: Ice Gym Location

The Ice Gym is located at the peak of *Glaseado Mountain*. Find the path up by traveling to *Montenevera*, proceeding south and going across the bridge.

3. Pass the Gym Test

This Gym test requires you to take on a, zero-battle, Time Trial race down the mountain.
You've 90-seconds to make it to the bottom, while making it through the checkpoints along the way.

Thankfully, simply hitting the inside of the flags still counts, so that makes the tighter corners easier for you to do.

Gym Battle:
Vs. Gym Leader Grusha

Pokémon	Level	Type	Weakness
	47	Ice / Grass	Fire, Flying, Rock, Steel
	47	Ice	Fighting, Fire, Rock, Steel
	47	Ice	Fighting, Fire, Rock, Steel
	48	Dragon / Flying / Ice	Dragon, Ice, Fairy, Rock

Lead with *Skeleridge* when fighting *Frosmoth*, as it's totally weak to Fire.

For *Beartic*, use some Speed boosts on your *Lucario* (or *Tinkaton*) and use your strongest **Fighting** or **Steel** moves.

Hit *Cetitan* with *Lucario*. Boost its Speed stat with your best Speed boost to help it get its moves in first.

Finally, bring out *Tinkaton* against *Altaria* as she only takes 50% damage from **Ice** and **Flying** moves, and is immune to **Dragon** moves!

Rewards:

- *8,640 money*
- *TM124* **Ice Spinner**
- *Ability to catch any level of Pokémon! Awesome!*

Endeavor
Fire Fa
The opposing Beartic used Earthquake!
GLASEADO GYM DEFEATED!
VICTORY ROAD

Elite Four
Becoming the Champion

With all eight of the main Gym leaders beaten and their respective badges earned, you can now turn your attention to beating the Elite Four and the current Paleda Pokémon Champion.

You need to make your way to the Pokémon League building, which is located in *Mesagoza*.

To find it, go left of the Pokémon Center, up the steps, go left, then the large gates in a cave behind the large gates (that are now open).

Once you exit the cave, go up the grassy path, heal at then save *before* you enter the large

Your Team

Make sure your Pokémon are a *minimum* of Level 62+ across the board as your opponents levels go up with each battle!

Our Picks

It's *imperative* that you go in with the most proficient Pokémon for the job.

Here's what Pokémon we used in each battle.

1st Battle

- Meowscarada,
- Gyarados,
- Azumarill.

2nd Battle

- Skeleridge,
- Dugtrio.

Caution

Once you begin battling the first of the Elite Four members, you **cannot stop** (but you *can* switch Pokémon and heal them in-between fights).

3rd Battle

- Dugtrio (Rock TT),
- Drednaw,
- Raichu.

4th Battle

- Sylveon,
- Tinkaton.

Final Battle

- Skeledirge,
- Meowscarada,
- Dugtrio (Rock TT).

However, before you can even get a chance to beat them, it's time for another obligatory test. Are you ready?…

Champion Assessment

You need to answer all of Rika's questions correctly to pass. The answers only have one correct answer, so make sure you pay attention to the questions (as they are based on circumstances that can differ).

To keep this simple, we'll only cover the answers you actually need to worry about (including the questions where the answers are tested with further questions!)

Q1. How did you get here today?

- I walked
- I rode on my Pokémon

The answer depends on whether you walked there, or got there by Pokémon!

Q2. Which school are you enrolled in?

- Naranja Academy
- Uva Academy

The answer depends on whether you are playing the Scarlet or Violet version of the game.

Scarlet players pick *Naranja Academy*, Violet players pick *Uva Academy*.

Q3. What brings you to the Pokémon League today?

- I came to become a Champion

Q4. What do you intend to do if you become a Champion?

- I want to become even stronger

Q5. Which Gym was the hardest?

- Glaseado Gym

Q6. What was the name of the Gym Leader?

- Grusha

Q7. What Pokemon did the Gym Leader use?

- Ice

Q8. What was your starter Pokémon?

- The Grass Cat Pokémon
- The Fire Croc Pokémon
- The Duckling Pokémon

This obviously depends on which one you picked right at the start!

Q9. What do you intend to do if you become a Champion?

- I want to become even stronger

Q10. Do you Like Pokémon?

- Yes

That's it! Stick to the answers we provide you (some of which will require you to remember some facts specific to how you played) and you'll pass this test and be granted access to the final Victory Road battles!

Let's go!

Elite Four:
Vs. Rika

Pokémon	Level	Type	Weakness
	57	Water / Ground	Grass x4
	57	Fire / Ground	Water x4, Ground
	57	Ground	Grass, Ice, Water
	57	Ground	Grass, Ice, Water
	58	Ground / Dark	Ice, Ground, Fairy, Water

Use an evolved **Grass-type** (such as *Meowscarada*) against *Whiscash*. The move **Flower Trick** is a solid choice here.

For *Camerupt*, use your strongest **Water-type** here in an effort to one-shot it (*before it can put you to sleep!*).

Use the same **Water-type** against *Donaphan* as it deals 2x damage. Be ready to cure it of any Poison attacks ASAP!

Use the same **Grass** and/or **Water-types** against *Dugtrio*. Just be very wary of its **Rock** moves as they're powerful!

Finally, *Clodsire* has a lot of annoying moves!
However, as you can Terastallize once per Elite Four battle, now's the time to use it!

A *Meowscarada* with **Energy Ball** will prove extremely handy in this battle as *Clodsire's* **Protect** move will mean it won't go down in one hit.

Reward:

- 12,296 money

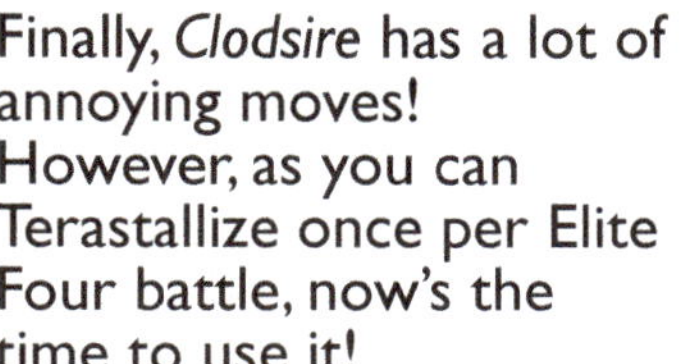

Elite Four:
Vs. Poppy

Pokémon	Level	Type	Weakness
	58		
	58		×4
	58		
	58		
Scarlet Exclusive			
	59		
Violet Exclusive			
	59		

Use a **Fire-type** such as *Skeleridge* (ideally with **Flamethrower** and/or the **Armor Cannon** moves) against *Copperajah*.

A *Dugtrio* with **Earthquake** will make very short work of *Magnezone* as it's extremely weak against **Ground-type** moves (and it's also immune to **Zap Cannon** and **Discharge**).

For *Bronzong*, either make sure your **Fire-type** is several levels higher, or use a **Dark/Ghost-type** to negate its powerful moves.

Use your **Fire-type** with **Flamethrower** again against *Corviknight*.

Finally, Terastallize your **Fire-type** to help make your life easier against either *Tera Tinkaton (Scarlet only)* or *Iron Treads (Violet only)*.

Your **Ground-type** can offer a "Plan B" if need be.

Reward:

- *12,296 money*

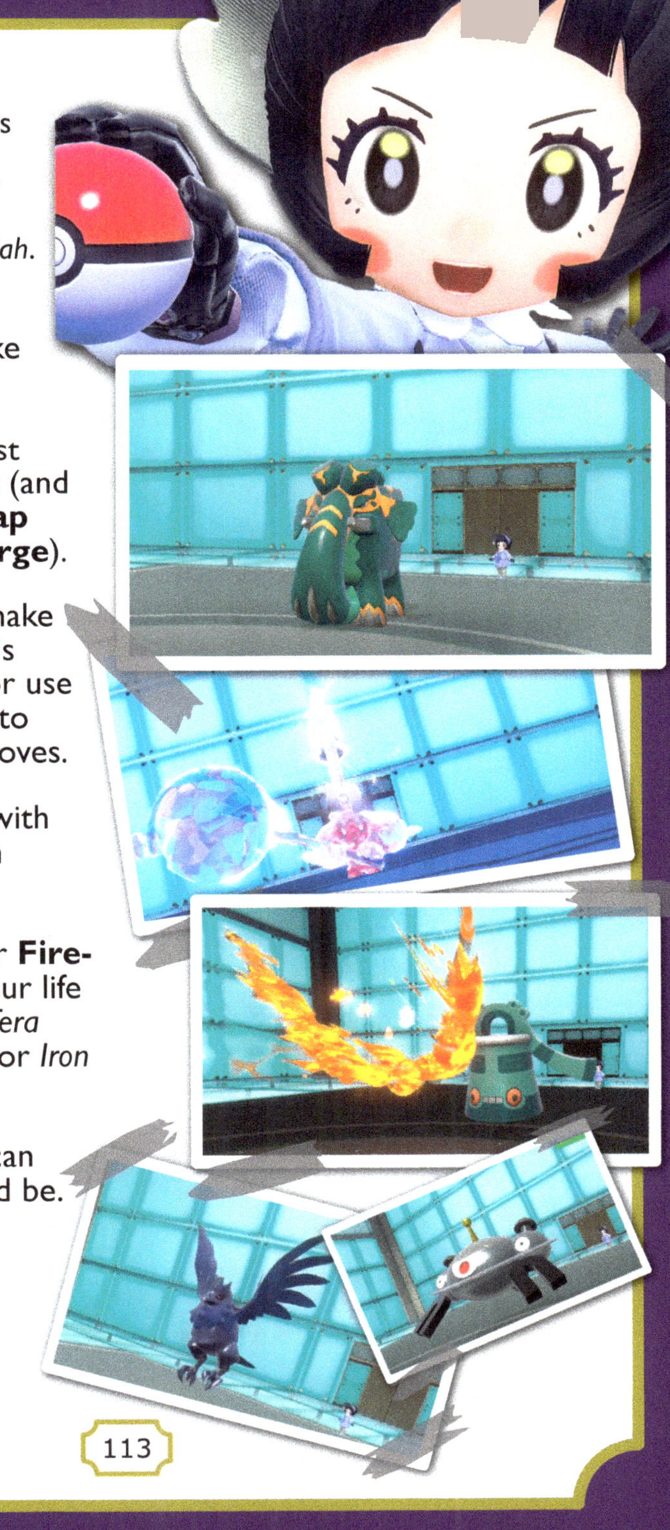

Elite Four:
Vs. Larry (Again)

Pokémon	Level	Type	Weakness
	59	Grass / Flying	Fire, Flying, Ice, Poison, Rock
	59	Steel / Flying	Electric, Rock, Water
	59	Electric / Flying	Ghost, Fairy, Ice, Rock
	59	Dark / Flying	Electric, Ice, Rock
	60	Fighting / Flying (Tera)	Electric, Fairy, Flying, Ice, Psychic

For most of these Pokémon, we used a **Rock-type** with a **Rock-Type** TT as well.

However, if you can re-spec your **Rock-type** to have the **Ice-type** TT, then it'll absolutely storm through these battles.

If you're playing the Violet version, then the **Rock/Electric-type** *Iron Thorns* is a very strong Pokémon for this particular series of battles.

An excellent back-up choice is any **Electric-type** with the **Fairy-type** move **Play** Rough (just keep them out of the fights against *Tropius* and *Altaria*).

Use a Speed boost to give your Pokémon the edge in battle and keep your Max healing items to hand, just in case Larry's Pokémon get the drop on you by sheer luck.

Reward:

- 12,720 money

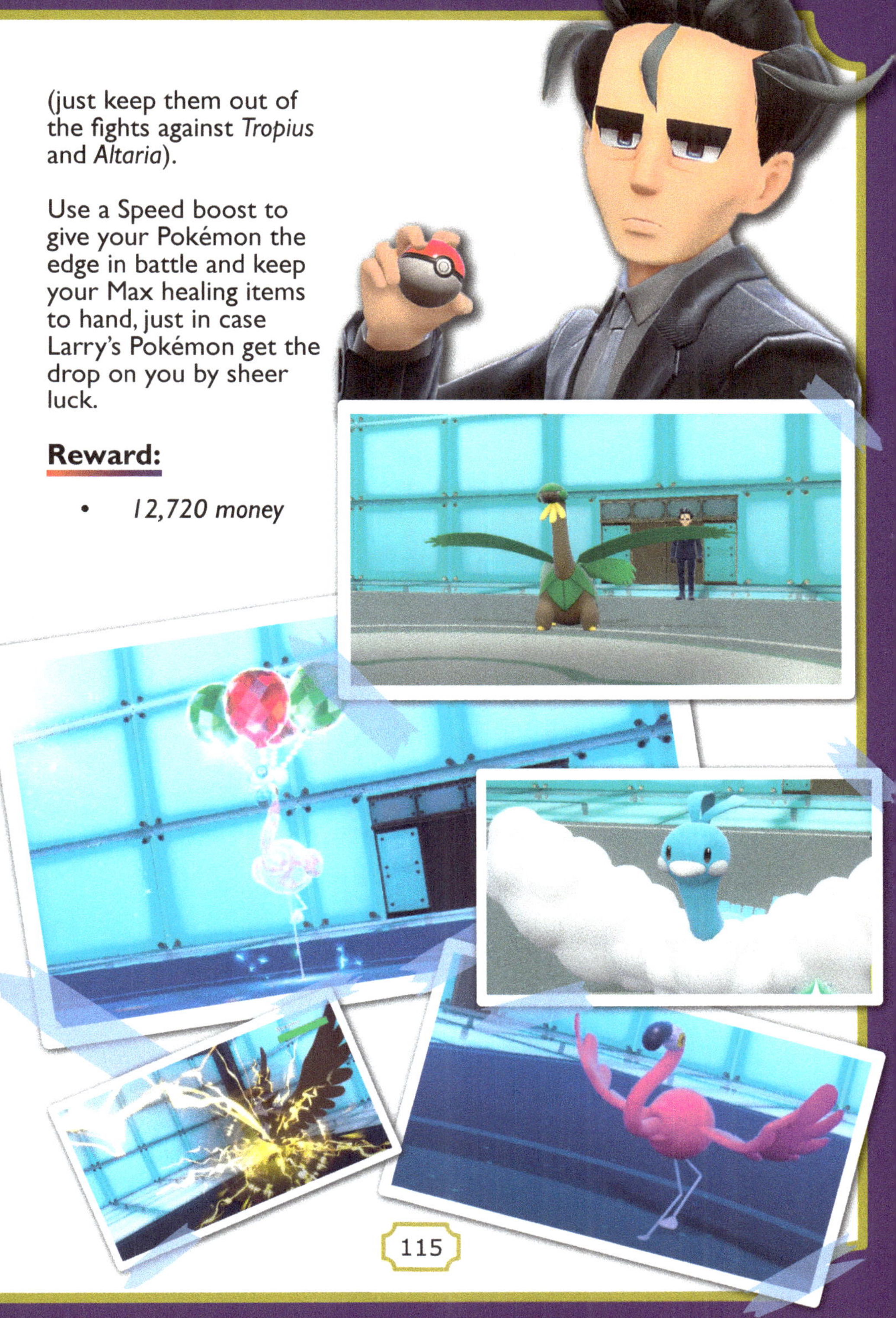

Pokémon	Level	Type	Weakness
	60	Flying / Dragon	Fire · Fairy · Ice · Rock
	60	Dragon	Dragon · Fairy · Ice
	60	Ground / Dragon	Fire · Ice · Ground · Fairy
	60	Grass / Dragon	Bug · Dragon · Fairy · Flying · Ice · Ground
	61	Ice / Dragon	Fire · Fairy · Fighting · Rock · Steel

The final battle of the Final Four is here!

We beat Hassel by mainly using *Sylveon* and started with **Calm Mind** (used 5-6 times), then a we used a combination of **Draining Kiss, Moonblast** to take out the rest. However…

Noivern is up first and is FAST and is quick to use **Super Fang**. It's also weak to **Rock** and **Ice-type** moves.

Haxorus is a pure **Dragon-type**. So, hit it quick with **Outrage**, or your strongest **Ice/Fairy-type** moves.

For *Dragalage*, use your fastest **Ice-type** to out-speed it. Keep your **Fairy-types** away from here.

For *Flapple*, **Ice** moves are the way for **4x damage!**

Finally, for *Baxcalibur*, use your strongest **Fairy-type** and note it's vulnerable right after using its **Glaive Rush** move.

Reward:

- 12,932 money

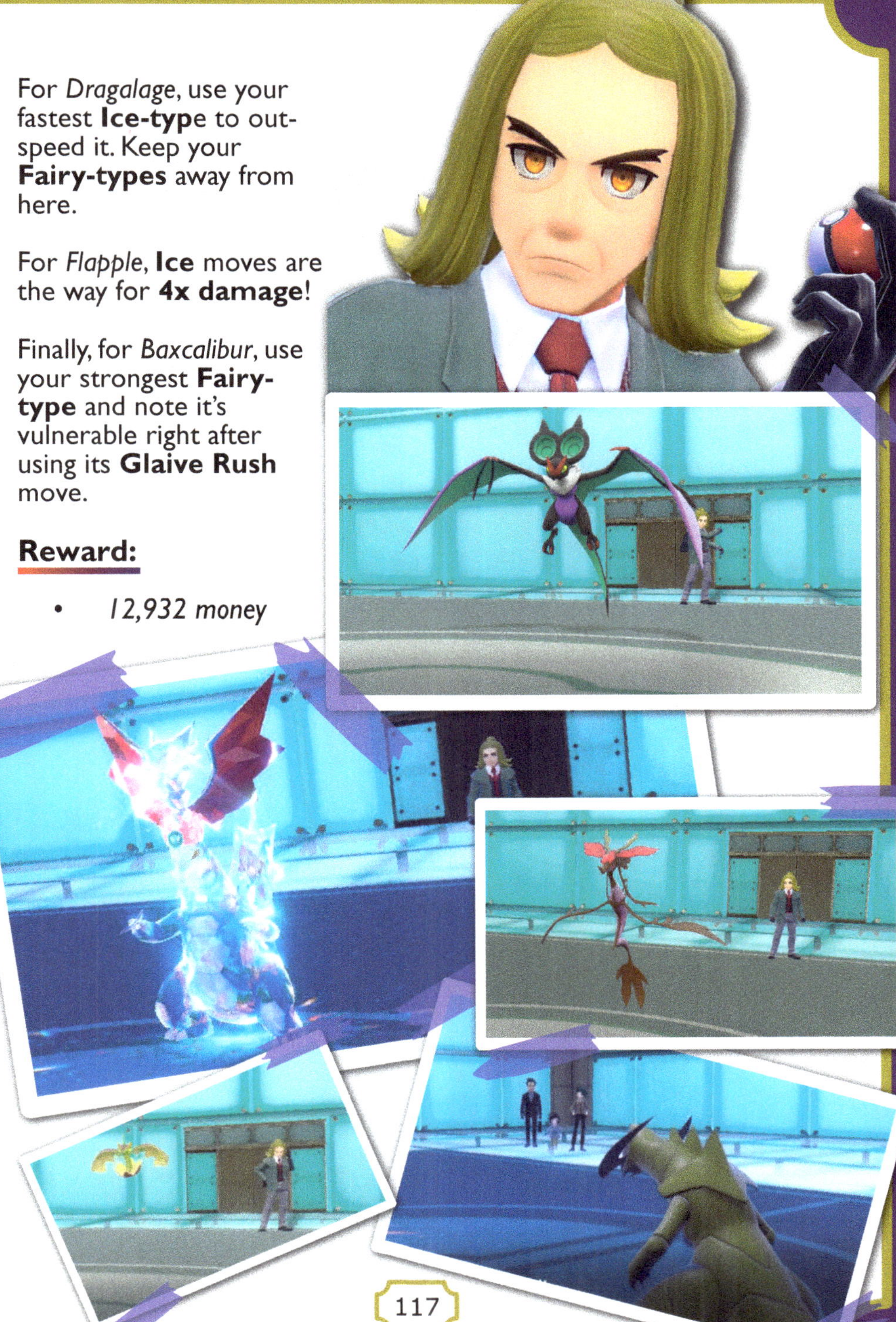

Pokémon	Level	Type	Weakness
	61		
	61		
	61		
	61		
	61		
	62		

It's time to take the top spot! For *Espathra*, bust out your strongest **Dark-type**, or **Bug-type** if it's fast.

Use your best **Fire-type** against *Gogoat*, with **Bug** as back-up. For *Veluza*, heal and re-use your strongest **Dark** and **Bug–types**.

When it comes to *Avalugg*, which is clearly weak against **Fire-types**. However, be wary of it's **Ground-type** move, **Earthquake**.

When it's *Kingambit's* turn, heal up your strongest **Fighting** and **Ground-type**s as it's a *very* strong opponent. Make sure your Pokémon are faster to maximize the odds of taking it out in one-shot (preferable).

Finally, Geeta uses a *Glimmora*, with a **Rock-type TT**.

Go **Ground-type** all the way (we used *Dugtrio* with a Rock TT). As it resists *both* **Tera Blast** and **Sludge Wave**.

Congrats! You're now the Top Pokémon Champion! But there's plenty more left to do…

Reward:

- *14,880 money*

Rival Nemona:
1st Battle: Tutorial

Pokémon	Level	Type	Weakness
	5	Grass	Bug, Fire, Flying, Ice, Poison
or			
	5	Fire	Ground, Rock, Water
or			
	5	Water	Electric, Grass

Nemona's first battle with you will automatically be weak to your chosen starting type.

Therefore, just pick your character's main elemental attack type and it'll be super effective against her Pokémon.

Reward:

- *Pokédex App*
- *500 money*

Rival Nemona:
2nd Battle: 1st Day of School

Pokémon	Level	Type	Weakness
Same Weak Starter	8	As Before	As Before
	9	⚡ / ⚡	

Nemona now introduces the first **Electric-type** opponent (*Pawmi*), as well rematching you against a Lv. 8 version of her starter Pokémon.

It's also your introduction to Terastallizaton..

Basically, Terastallizing a Pokémon either alters its Type, or enhances its existing one (if the type is the same), by making that move more powerful! Simply attack with your strongest elemental type to win. Nice and easy.

Reward:

- *530 money*

Rival Nemona:
3rd Battle: Enter the 3rd Gym

Pokémon	Level	Type	Weakness
	21		
	21		
	22		
or			
	22		
or			
	22		

Nemona now's brings a new Pokémon into her team, a **Rock-type** called *Rockruff*.

It's resistant to **Fire-types**. However, you should hopefully have a *Diglett/Dugtrio* by now as this Pokémon will easily beat the first two of Nemona's (and will also do really well if she has *Croclaor*), and they were very easy to find on your way to the first Gym.

Once *Rockruff* and *Pawmo* have been dispatched, it's time to ready your starter Pokémon to take on her final Pokémon.

TT-your Pokémon to boost its stats and this fight will be over quickly.

Rewards:

- 1320 money
- 3x Heals

Rival Nemona:
4th Battle: After the 5th Gym

Pokémon	Level	Type	Weakness
	36		
	36		
	36		
	37		
or			
	37		
or			
	37		

Your best **Ground-type** Pokémon (we used *Dugtrio*) will work wonders against her *Lycanroc* (2x damage), less so against *Goomy* (1x damage), and *Pawmo* (2x damage).

If you have a decent **Ice-type**, then feel free to use it against *Goomy*, but by the time we got to this fight, our *Dugtrio* was *far* stronger than Level 36.

As long as you still have your evolved starter (which we really hope you do!), then you can revert to using it against the now - fully-evolved - opponent Pokémon.

Just keep in mind that they are now dual-types, so pay attention to their additional strengths (and weaknesses) to make light work of them in this fight. You've got this!

Rewards:

- *TM0171*
  Tera Blast

- *4,440 money*

Rival Nemona:

5th Battle: Enter the 7th Gym

Pokémon	Level	Type	Weakness
	42	Normal	Fighting, Grass, Ground, Ice, Water
	42	Ghost	Ghost, Fairy, Ice
	42	Electric, Fighting	Fairy, Ground, Psychic
	43	Grass, Dark	Bug, Fairy, Fighting, Fire, Flying, Ice, Poison
or			
	43	Fire, Ghost	Dark, Ghost, Ground, Rock, Water
or			
	43	Water, Fighting	Electric, Fairy, Flying, Grass, Psychic

This is effectively a re-match against her last set of Pokémon (with the only difference being that the *Goomy* evolved into a *Sliggoo*).

However, other than being more powerful, it's *still* a pure **Dragon-type**, so you can simply re-use the exact same tactics that you used in the fourth battle to end this fight just as quickly!

Rewards:

- *Max Potion x3*
- *7,740 money*

Rival Nemona:

6th Battle: Beat Geeta

Pokémon	Level	Type	Weakness
	65		
	65		
	65		
	65		
	65		
And, finally against Meowscarada, Skeledirge, or Quaquaval			
	66		

You can use the same team as you used before in this - the sixth and final - battle. Just make sure you're leveled up to *at least* Level-66 (or more)!

However, as she also brought an *Orthworm* and *Dudunsparce* to the party, it's worth taking a closer look at before you battle them in the arena.

Orthworm is a **Steel-type**, so your strongest **Fighting** or **Ground-type** moves will do the trick nicely in this fight.

When you're up against *Dudunsparce*, the only real option you have here are **Fighting-type** moves.

For reference, a level 75-*Lucario* can be caught at *Dalizapa Passage*. Strong enough against at least half of her team.

Ready your starter Pokémon for the final match to finish off the **Victory Road** story-line completely! Well done!

Lv. 27
Torkoal
POISONED
Slam 20/20
Mud Shot 14/15
Poison Jab 20/20
Poison Tail
TERASTALLIZE!
9/30
Send Pokémon   Recall Pokémon   Give Up
13/30
The opposing Dachsbun used Baby-Doll Eyes!

Starfall Street

You Vs. Team Star

The next path you can take through the world is a series of battles against a range of new "boss battles." There's a total of five "crews" to beat and, naturally, each crew specializes in a particular type of Pokémon.

What makes these fights stand out is that, once you've beaten the multiple waves of lower-level grunts, the crew's boss will make an appearance in a funky car-like Pokémon type known as a *Starmobile*! You now need to pay attention to this vehicular addition, as it can drive around and get in your way during a battle!

As with the Victory Road gym battles, we'll give you the benefit of our hindsight and share with you our suggestions on what types will be best suited to take into each battle with you, along with the Pokémon that you should have ready for the all-new "Star Barrage" challenge that awaits you at each Crew's base...

Starfall Street

Dark Crew

Your Goals:

- Level up Pokémon team to Lv. 21+,
- Locate the Dark Crew
- Attack their base,
- Fight the Crew Leader.

1: Build your team

Dark types are, naturally, weak against **Fighting**. They're also weak to **Bug and Fairy-types**.

We recommend the following:

- Kirlia (Psychic/Fairy),
- Pawmo (Electric/Fighting),
- Tauros (Fighting).

2: Dark Crew Location

The Dark Crew is located off a trail south-east from the town of *Cascarrafa* (which is located west of *Mesagoza*).

3. Attacking the Crew's Base via "Star Barrage"

Each base requires you to first defeat the guard(s) and then you must take your **first three** Pokémon into the base and have them defeat **30** opposing Pokémon using the auto-battling feature - known as a Star Barrage.

You must send out your first three Pokémon into the base. You'll notice small groups of opposing Pokémon appear around the base.

You've got 10-minutes in which to defeat those 30 Pokémon, but with the right team at the helm, it's a *very* generous time-limit, so don't sweat it.

Top Tip!

Just before hitting the 30 mark, return back to Clive at the entrance and heal up as you go straight into the leader fight once all 30 are defeated!

Team Grunt Battle

You first need to take care of the Grunt guarding the gate. Use your best **Electric**, **Fairy**, **Ice**, or **Ground** moves. Once it's been defeated, it's time to arrange your top three **Fighting/Bug/Fairy-types** (in this order).

Pokémon	Level	Type	Weakness
	20		

Pokémon	Level	Type	Weakness
	20		
	20		x4
	20		
	20		
	20		
	20		
	20		

Star Barrage

Once you make it inside the Crew's camp, it's time to get ready to send your Pokémon out to battle.

The table on the page opposite provides you with a list of the different **Dark-types** you'll find wandering around the Crew base.

Keep pressing **R** to send all three out to battle, and head back to the entrance to heal up (however, if your team isn't clearing the field as-is, then your team won't be strong enough for the leader).

Once all 30 have been defeated, up the Speed stat on your strongest Pokemon and then it's time to take on the Crew's leader…

Pokémon	Level	Type	Weakness
	21	👁 🔷	✊ *x4* 🔥 🟫
	20	👁	🟢 🟣 ✊

It should be very easy to one-shot the *Pawniard* by using your strongest **Fighting** move (as it's 4x the damage).

However, the *Segin Starmobile* is where you'll find the difficulty ramping up quite a bit.

Bring your strongest **Fighting** and **Fairy-types** out so they can minimize the damage taken by its quick and painful moves!

It has a **very** fast Speed level, allowing it to potentially get in *multiple* moves on a single turn (hence boosting the speed of your strongest Pokémon earlier).

It also frequently uses **Intimidate** or **Snarl** to drop your attack level before you can move and **Wicked Torque**

It's also partial to using **Metal Sound**, causing your Sp. Def to fall sharply, which **Snarl** then causes *extra* damage from! Ouch!

Therefore, be ready to heal often as it will often hit you twice per turn.

Be ready to switch out Pokémon if need be as this can be a tough battle if you go in at a similar level. Otherwise, keep the pressure up to win!

Rewards:

- *Approx. 5000 LP*
- *TM062 **Foul Play***
- *Loads of new TM recipes and materials.*

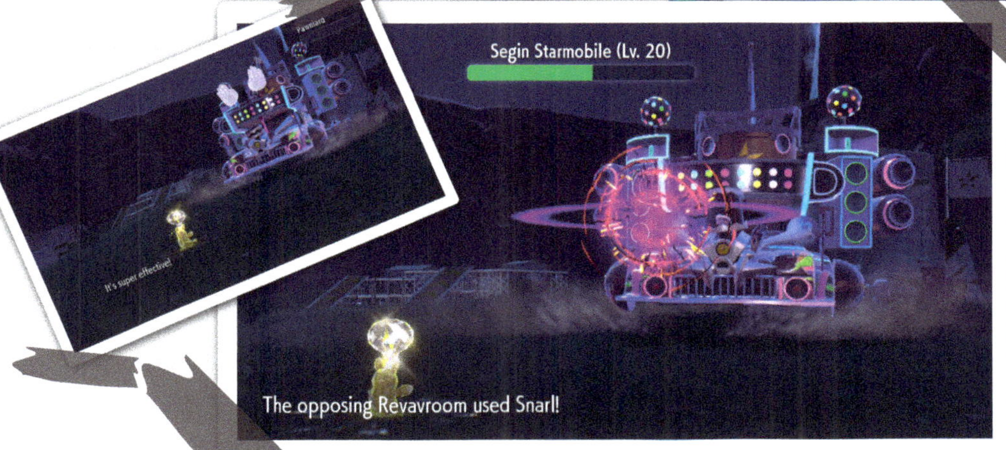

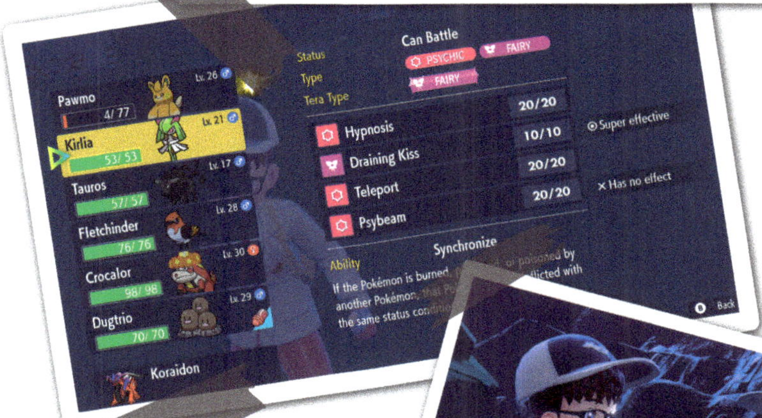

Starfall Street

Fire Crew

Your Goals:

- Level up Pokémon team to Lv. 27+,
- Locate the Fire Crew
- Attack their base,
- Fight the Crew Leader.

1: Build your team

Naturally **Water**-types are a solid choice against Fire. They're also weak to **Rock and Ground-types** (less-so Ground-types).

We recommend the following:

- Drednaw (Water/Rock),
- Dugtrio (Ground/Rock TT),
- Psyduck (Water).

2: Fire Crew Location

The Fire Crew is located not far from the Pokémon Center that's in the *East Province (Area One)*.

3. Attacking the Crew's Base via "Star Barrage"

As before, you must first defeat the guard(s) and then you must take your **first three** Pokémon into the base and have them defeat **30** opposing Pokémon.

You must send out your first three Pokémon into the base. You'll notice small groups of opposing Pokémon appear around the base.

You've got 10-minutes in which to defeat those 30 Pokémon, but with the right team at the helm, it's a *very* generous time-limit, so don't sweat it.

Top Tip!

Just before hitting the 30 mark, return back to Clive at the entrance and heal up as you go straight into the leader fight once all 30 are defeated!

Team Grunt Battle

You first need to take care of the Grunt guarding the gate. Use your best **Water**, **Ground**, **Rock**, or **Fighting** moves.

Once it's been defeated, it's time to arrange your top three **Rock/Water/Ground-types** (in this order).

Now approach the base and begin the next Star Barrage.

Pokémon	Level	Type	Weakness
	25	Fire / Dark	Fighting, Ground, Rock, Water

Pokémon	Level	Type	Weakness
	25	Fire	Ground, Rock, Water
	25	Fire / Dark	Fighting, Ground, Rock, Water
	25	Fire / Ground	Ground, Water
	25	Fire	Ground, Rock, Water

Star Barrage

Once you make it inside the Crew's camp, it's time to get ready to send your Pokémon out to battle.

The table on the page opposite provides you with a list of the different fire-types you'll find wandering around the Crew base.

Keep pressing **R** to send all three out to battle, and head back to the entrance to heal up (however, if your team isn't clearing the field as-is, then your team won't be strong enough for the leader).

Once all 30 have been defeated, up the Speed stat on your strongest Pokemon and then it's time to take on the Crew's leader…

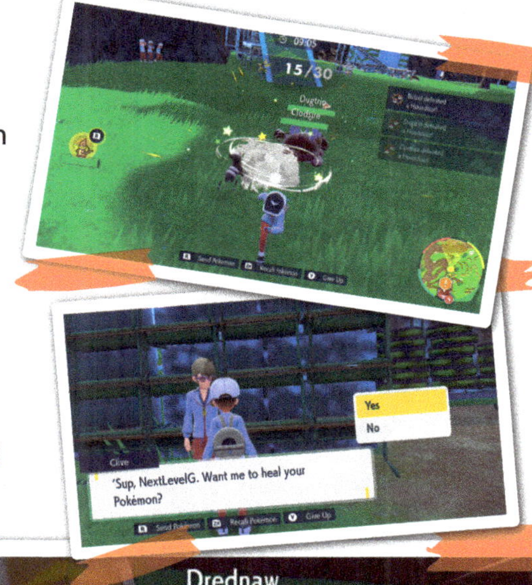

Crew Battle:
Vs. Crew Leader Mela

Pokémon	Level	Type	Weakness
	27	🔥	
	26	🔥	

You'll want to lead with your Rock-type as it won't be affected by the **Sunny Day** move.

We used our *Dugtrio* (with **Rock** TT) to get through the first fight.

When it comes to fighting the Starmobile, it boosts its speed after every turn.

You also need to be cautious of its tendency to use **Lazing Torque** (which usually causes Burn), so be ready to use some **Burn Heals** as and when they're needed.

Drednaw is a solid choice, but be ready to swap it out as it can be badly hurt by **Burn** and swapping out a Pokémon that's negatively impacted by a debuff (such as **Burn**) cancels that defbuff.

Ultimately, be ready to heal and swap around Pokémon as required and this isn't *too* difficult a fight.

Rewards:

- *Approx. 5000 LP*
- *TM038* **Flame Charge**
- *Loads of new TM recipes and materials.*

Schedar Starmobile (Lv. 26)
The opposing Revavroom's Speed rose!
Schedar Starmobile (Lv. 26)
The opposing Revavroom used Blazing Torque!
Dugtrio
69/76
Dugtrio used Rock Tomb!
Schedar Starmobile (Lv. 26)
The opposing Revavroom used Blazing Torque!
TEAM STAR'S FIRE CREW DEFEATED!
★ STARFALL STREET ★

Starfall Street
Poison Crew

Your Goals:

- *Level up Pokémon team to Lv. 33+,*
- *Locate the Poison Crew*
- *Attack their base,*
- *Fight the Crew Leader.*

1: Build your team

Ground and **Psychic-types** are a solid choice against **Poison**. Our high-level *Dugtrio* (with it's **Rock-type** TT) once again worked wonders.

We recommend the following:

- *Dugtrio (Ground/Rock TT),*
- *Phanpy (Ground),*
- *Clodsire (Poison/Steel).*

2: Poison Crew Location

The Poison Crew is located north of *Zapapico*, found in the *Tagtree Thicket* area (west of *East Province (Area Three)*.

3. Attacking the Crew's Base via "Star Barrage"

As before, you must first defeat the guard(s) and then you must take your **first three** Pokémon into the base and have them defeat **30** opposing Pokémon.

You must send out your first three Pokémon into the base. You'll notice small groups of opposing Pokémon appear around the base.

You've got 10-minutes in which to defeat those 30 Pokémon, but with the right team at the helm, it's a *very* generous time-limit, so don't sweat it.

Top Tip!

Just before hitting the 30 mark, return back to Clive at the entrance and heal up as you go straight into the leader fight once all 30 are defeated!

Trainer Battle

Make sure you leading with your strongest **Ground-type** here and if they're at level 33+, then there shouldn't be any issues taking out both the *Gulpin* and the *Shroodle*.

Pokémon	Level	Type	Weakness
	30		
	31		

Pokémon	Level	Type	Weakness
	31		
	31		
	31		
	31		
	31		

Pokémon	Level	Type	Weakness
	31		
	31		
	31		
	31		
	31		x4
	31		
	31		
	31		

Star Barrage

Once you make it inside the Crew's camp, it's time to get ready to send your Pokémon out using auto-battle.

The tables on the page opposite (and above) provides you with a list of the different **Poison-types** you'll find wandering around the Crew base. 30 of which you must dispatch in under 10-minutes.

Pokémon	Level	Type	Weakness
	32	Ground / Dark	Ground
	33	Ground / Steel	Ground x4 / Fire
	32	Ground	Ground / Fairy
	32	Ground	Ground / Fairy

Firstly, lead with your strongest **Ground-type** (as *Skuntnak* is half **Dark-type**).

This is where our *Dugtrio* came back into its own again as it also deals a whopping **4x damage** to the regular *Vevavroom*, so that shouldn't bee *too* difficult of a fight.

However, it's worth making sure that you've enough **Antidotes** to hand and heal up with potions as required.

For *Muk*, once again your Ground-type should be leading the way.

However, the second *Vevavroom* is a *Navi Starmobile* and has a few tricks.

Flame Charge and **Spin Out** can be a real pain to deal with. Therefore, using your *Whiscash* here is *very* helpful as it's immune to *both* of these annoying moves.

Rewards:

- *Approx. 5000 LP*

- *TM102* **Gunk Shot**

- *Loads of new TM recipes and materials.*

Tera (Fire)

Starfall Street

Fairy Crew

Your Goals:

- Level up Pokémon team to Lv. 51+,
- Locate the Fairy Crew
- Attack their base,
- Fight the Crew Leader.

1: Build your team

Poison and **Steel-types** are a solid choice against **Fairy** Pokémon. There's a level-55 *Tera Revavroom* nearby (which is both **Poison** *and* **Steel**!

We recommend the following:

- Tera Revavroom (Poison/Steel),
- Tinkatuff (Fairy/Steel),
- Bronzong (Psychic/Steel).

2: Fighting Crew Location

Found north of *Glaseado Mountain* in the *North Province* (Area Three), just after the river.

3. Attacking the Crew's Base via "Star Barrage"

As before, you must first defeat the guard(s) and then you must take your **first three** Pokémon into the base and have them defeat **30** opposing Pokémon.

You must send out your first three Pokémon into the base. You'll notice small groups of opposing Pokémon appear around the base.

You've got 10-minutes in which to defeat those 30 Pokémon, but with the right team at the helm, it's a *very* generous time-limit, so don't sweat it.

Top Tip!

Just before hitting the 30 mark, return back to Clive at the entrance and heal up as you go straight into the leader fight once all 30 are defeated!

Trainer Battle

Make sure you leading with your strongest **Poison-type** here and if they're at Lv. 51+, then there shouldn't be any issues taking out both the *Morgrem* and the *Hattrem*.

Pokémon	Level	Type	Weakness
	48		
	49		

Pokémon	Level	Type	Weakness
	49		
	49		
	49		
	49		
	49		

Pokémon	Level	Type	Weakness
	49		
	49		
	49		
	49		
	49		
	49		
	49		
	49		

Star Barrage

Once you make it inside the Crew's camp, it's time to get ready to send your Pokémon out using auto-battle.

The tables on the page opposite (and above) provides you with a list of the different **Fairy-types** you'll find wandering around the Crew base. 30 of which you must dispatch in under 10-minutes.

Pokémon	Level	Type	Weakness
	50	Water / Fairy	Electric / Grass / Ground
	50	Steel / Fairy	Ground / Rock
	51	Fairy	Ground / Rock
	50	Fairy	Ground / Rock

Firstly, lead with your strongest **Poison-type** (as Azumarill is half **Fairy-type**). However, stick to using **Poison** moves against the Azumarill as **Steel** only does 1x damage.

Ultimately, we mainly focused on using our Level 55 *Tera Revavroom* to deal the hurt in this battle, with our *Tinkaton* and *Bronzong* only coming out if we needed to get rid of a stat-affecting attack.

While the **Fairy-type** *Ruchbah Starmobile* can throw out a few arena-affecting moves, it's mainly its **Magical Torque** move (which hits hard *and* can cause **Confuse** to you too!).

So, switch and heal your Pokémon team as needed.

Rewards:

- Approx. 5000 LP
- TM079 **Dazzling Gleam**
- Loads of new TM recipes and materials.

Tera (Fairy)

Starfall Street
Fighting Crew

Your Goals:

- *Level up Pokémon team to Lv. 57+,*
- *Locate the Fighting Crew*
- *Attack their base,*
- *Fight the Crew Leader.*

1: Build your team

Fairy, Flying, and **Psychic-types** are a solid choice against **Fighting** Pokémon.

We recommend the following:

- *Tinkaton (Fairy/Steel)*
- *Mimikyu (Ghost/Fairy),*
- *Gyarados (Water/Flying).*

2: Fighting Crew Location

The Fighting Crew is located in the *North Province (Area Two)*. Hopefully you've unlocked the flying ability to make it *much* easier to reach.

3. Attacking the Crew's Base via "Star Barrage"

As before, you must first defeat the guard(s) and then you must take your **first three** Pokémon into the base and have them defeat **30** opposing Pokémon.

You must send out your first three Pokémon into the base. You'll notice small groups of opposing Pokémon appear around the base.

You've got 10-minutes in which to defeat those 30 Pokémon, but with the right team at the helm, it's a *very* generous time-limit, so don't sweat it.

Top Tip!

Just before hitting the 30 mark, return back to Clive at the entrance and heal up as you go straight into the leader fight once all 30 are defeated!

Crew Grunt Battle

We used *Bronzong's* strongest Psychic attack moves to deal a whopping 4x damage to the *Croagunk* and a very respectable 2x damage to the *Primeape*. Easy.

Pokémon	Level	Type	Weakness
	54		
	55		

Pokémon	Level	Type	Weakness
	55		x4
	55		
	55		
	55		
	55		

Pokémon	Level	Type	Weakness
	55	Fighting	Fairy, Flying, Psychic
	55	Fighting, Flying	Electric, Fairy, Flying, Ice, Psychic
	55	Fighting	Fairy, Flying, Psychic
	55	Fighting, Fairy	Fairy, Flying, Ghost
	55	Fighting	Fairy, Flying, Psychic
	55	Fighting	Fairy, Flying, Psychic
	55	Poison, Fighting	Flying, Ground, Psychic

Star Barrage

Once you make it inside the Crew's camp, it's time to get ready to send your Pokémon out using auto-battle.

The tables on the page opposite (and above) provides you with a list of the different **Fighting-types** you'll find wandering around the Crew base.

30 of which you must dispatch in under 10-minutes.

Pokémon	Level	Type	Weakness
	55		
	55		
	56		
	56		
	55		

Enter this battle with a party consisting of two **Fairy**, two **Flying**, one **Psychic**, and a **Ground-type**.

Toxicroak takes 4x damage from **Psychic** moves, but its **Sucker Punch** move hits you hard.

For *Passimian*, use a Fairy or Psychic-type as **Flying-types** could get KO'd by **Rock Tomb**.

When against *Lucario*, use your **Ground-type** to take it out quickly, so hit it hard and fast.

Using a *Mimikyu* against *Annihilape* means you are able to take this out super-quick as it's vulnerable to both **Ghost** and **Fairy** moves.

Finally, the *Caph* Starmobile is **very** strong!

Its **Stamina** ability means *all* **Physical-type** attacks simply boost its defenses!

It's main move, **Combat Torque** will likely cause Paralysis. **Spin Out** is a strong **Steel** attack that lowers your speed.

TT your strongest **Psychic-type** and stick to using Special Attacks!

You **must** hit it hard *and* fast to ensure the win.

Rewards:

- *Approx. 8,000 LP*
- *TM167* **Close Combat**
- *Loads of new TM recipes and materials.*

Starfall Street

"Clive" Fight

Your Goals:

- *Level up Pokémon team to Lv. 62+,*
- *Locate Clive,*
- *Fight and defeat Clive.*

1: Build your team

"Clive" isn't messing around. He uses a wide-variety of different types, so you *really* need to go into this battle prepared.

> ### Top Tip!
>
> If you picked a **Fire-type** as your starting type, then make sure you bring your strongest one out here. It'll come in *very* handy…

So, let's take a closer look at the team *we* used to beat him.

We recommend the following:

- *Baxacalibur (Dragon/Ice)*
- *Skeledirge (Fire/Ghost),*
- *Pawmot (Electric/Fighting),*
- *Dugtrio (Ground/Steel).*

These four took us through the whole battle (*Dugtrio* for one battle, *Baxacalibur* for two battles, and our main Pokemon *Skeledirge* won us three battles).

We also took in the following two Pokemon as "Plan B" back-ups (which we never needed).

- *Lucario (Fighting/Steel),*
- *Talonflame (Fire/Flying).*

2: Locating Clive

Clive can be found at the front of your Academy (*during the day only*).

Crew Battle: Vs. "Clive"

Pokémon	Level	Type	Weakness
	60	(Normal) (Fairy)	(Grass) (Poison)
	60	(Grass) (Ice)	(Grass) (Fighting) (Fire) x4 (Flying) (Poison) (Rock) (Steel)
	60	(Water) (Flying)	(Electric) (Rock)
	60	(Dark) (Fire)	(Fighting) (Ground) (Rock) (Water)
	60	(Grass) (Poison)	(Ice) (Fire) (Flying) (Fairy)
	60	(Ghost)	(Ghost) (Dark)
Skeleridge, Meowscarada, or Quaquaval	61		The opposite of your starter.

We went up against his *Oranguru* with *Baxcalibur*. Hit it hard with your strongest **Dark-type** moves.

We used our high-level *Skeledirge* (our starter-type) against his *Abomasnow* for 4x damage. If you also chose a **Fire-starter**, **Terastallize it now!** (trust us on this one).

For *Gyarados* we rocked out our strongest **Electric-type** and gave it a **Speed boost** to give it a helpful edge in this battle.

For *Houndoom*, we used our go-to **Ground-type**, *Dugtrio*. We had given ours Rock-type moves which worked *very* well for us during this battle.

We, once again, used our high-level *Skeledirge* against his *Amoonguss*. **Fire Blast** is able to one-shot this opponent.

For *Polteageist*, we hit it with your best Dark-type moves from *Baxcalibur*.

Finally, you'll go up against the opposite of your starter Pokémon. Should be a very easy win here.

Reward:

- *13420 in money.*

Starfall Street
"Cassiopeia" Fight

Your Goals:

- *Level up Pokémon team to Lv. 63+,*
- *Locate Cassiopeia,*
- *Fight and defeat Cassiopeia.*

1: Build your team

"Cassiopeia" isn't as challenging as the *Director* was, as she uses only single-type Pokémon in battle.

If you've been following our guide throughout, then you should have a very solid team in place by now. In fact, you can re-use most of the team you used against the *Director* against Cassiopeia too!

So, let's take a closer look at the team *we* used to beat her.

We recommend the following:

- *Skeledirge (Fire/Ghost),*
- *Pawmot (Electric/Fighting),*
- *Dugtrio (Ground/Steel),*
- *Clodsire (Ground/Poison).*

These four took us through the whole battle (*Dugtrio* for two battles, *Pawmot* for two battles, *Clodsire* for one, and our main starter *Skeledirge* won us one battle).

We also took in the following Pokémon as "Plan B" back-ups (which we never needed).

- *Lucario (Fighting/Steel).*

2: Locating Cassiopeia

Cassiopeia can be found in the schoolyard of your Academy (*during the night-time only*).

Pokémon	Level	Type	Weakness
	62	Dark	Grass, Fairy, Fighting
	62	Electric	Ground
	62	Fire	Ground, Rock, Water
	62	Grass	Bug, Fire, Flying, Ice, Poison
	62	Water	Electric, Grass
	63	Fairy	Poison, Steel

Top Tip!

Giving your team an attack boost item to hold *before* starting this battle counters her use of **Baby-doll eyes**.

Firstly, we used *Pawmot's* strongest **Fighting-type** moves against *Umbreon*. One-to-two hits was all it took and the battle was over.

Against Jolteon, we TT'd our *Dugtrio* and used our strongest **Ground-type** moves on it. Another quick and easy fight.

For *Flareon*, we stuck with *Dugtrio* and used our strongest **Ground** and **Rock-type** moves (we had a **Rock-type** TT).

We busted out our Fire-starter, turned fire-machine *Skeledirge* against her *Leafeon*. Wasn't even a fair fight.

We brought our *Pawmo* back out to play against her *Vaporeon* and used its strongest **Electric-type** moves against it.

Finally, our *Clodsire* came out and busted out his strongest **Poison-type** moves against her *Sylveon*.

Reward:

- *TM169* **Draco Meteor.**

169

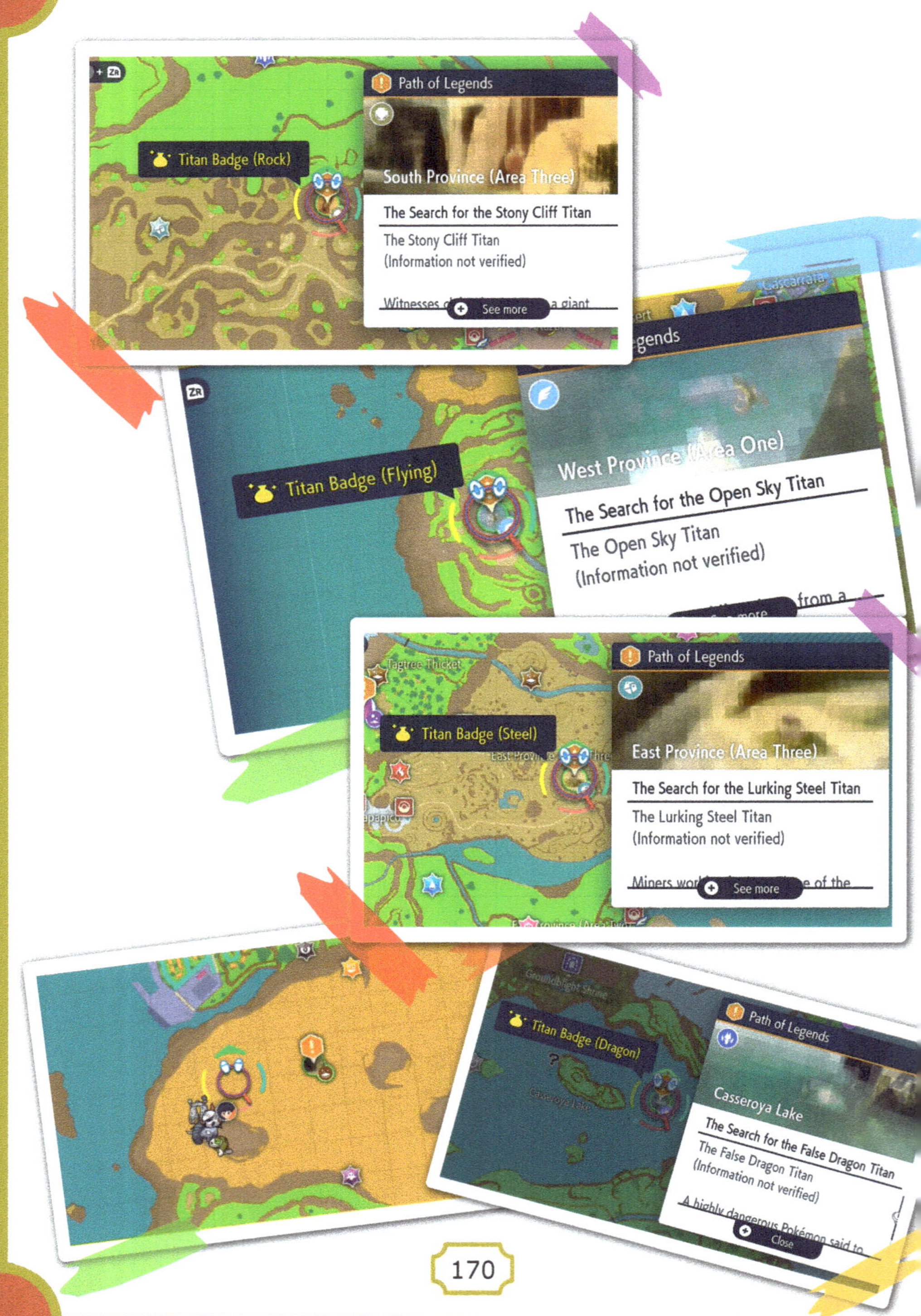
Titan Badge (Rock)
Path of Legends
South Province (Area Three)
The Search for the Stony Cliff Titan
The Stony Cliff Titan
(Information not verified)
Witnesses a giant
See more
Titan Badge (Flying)
legends
West Province (Area One)
The Search for the Open Sky Titan
The Open Sky Titan
(Information not verified)
from a
Tagtree Thicket
Titan Badge (Steel)
Path of Legends
East Province (Area Three)
The Search for the Lurking Steel Titan
The Lurking Steel Titan
(Information not verified)
Miners work the of the
See more
Titan Badge (Dragon)
Path of Legends
Casseroya Lake
The Search for the False Dragon Titan
The False Dragon Titan
(Information not verified)
A highly dangerous Pokémon said to
Close

Path of Legends
You Vs. Titan Pokémon!

The third, and final, key path available to you are the battles against the five hidden Titan Pokémon.

While you're welcome to tackle them in the order you want to, it's *highly* recommended that you tackle them in the order that we present them in this guide. They each have a distinctly different Level that's pre-determined, so, unless you're *intentionally* trying to make the game harder, our suggested order provides a more manageable - and natural - progression through the game.

Finally, and most importantly, defeating each Titan unlocks a new travel ability for your Legendary Pokémon that's been allowing you to ride on top of it.

The following table details what order to tackle them in and what travel ability beating them unlocks:

Titan	Location	Travel Ability
Stony Cliff Titan	Cliff region, north-west of *Artazon*.	**Dash**
Open Sky Titan	Far-west, south of *Asado Desert*.	**Surf**
Lurking Steel Titan	Gravel area, north-west of *Levincia*.	**Jump**
Quaking Earth Titan	Asado Desert, south of *Porto Marinada*.	**Glide**
False Dragon Titan	Far-eastern island, *Casseroya Lake*.	**Climb**

Legend Battle:
Vs. Stony Cliff Titan

Pokémon	Level	Type	Weakness
	16		x4 x4

Thankfully, Klawf is a relatively easy battle (as long as you're Lv. 17+ and pick a Pokémon that it's weak to).

To prove how simple this battle is, we chose not to use a **Grass** or **Water-type** (which both cause 4x damage).

We managed to ace it first-try with a Lv. 19 *Diglett* using **Ground-based** moves.

Note

These battles are all split into two different rounds, with a gap in-between which allows you to heal, or switch up your Pokémon.

Round One

Straight out the gate, we hit it hard with a regular Ground-based move, **Bulldoze**, taking off almost ½ of its energy!

Remember to Terastallize your Pokémon to get the most out of your attacks.

It'll use **Rock Smash** to lower your defense to physical attacks, and **Rock Tomb** to drop your speed.

Two - three hits maximum is all it should take to trigger round two of this battle.

Round Two

Heal up, give your Pokémon an Attack boost, then drop down to begin the battle.

The *Titan Klawf* now deals extra damage per-hit. However, *Arven* turns up and deals 4x damage with his **Water-type**. Thanks *Arven!*

It'll now use **Anger Shell** to buff up its Attack, Sp. Atk, and Speed stats, but it's now 2 v 1 and it doesn't stand a chance.

Its **Vice Grip** attack will deal OK damage, so heal if it takes off more than 25%.

Heal when needed and this battle should be over in a few minutes.

Reward:

- **Dash**.

Legend Battle:
Vs. Open Sky Titan

Pokémon	Level	Type	Weakness
	19		

The path leading up to the battle is fraught with rolling boulders. Ride up there on your Pokémon transport and if you get hit, you *won't* take any damage!

Bombirdier, the Open Sky Titan, isn't too hard to defeat (again, as long as your chosen Pokémon are of the same - or higher - level, and of the type it is weakest to).

Round One

Now, our main choice was unconventional, as *we* used our Lv. 27 *Dugtrio* (a **Ground**-type) that had a **Rock-type** Terastallization and it had some hard-hitting **Rock** moves (**Tomb Stone** in this case).

If you're of a more equal level that we were by this battle, then you'll need to play a bit more cautiously as your damage won't be as significant as ours was for this fight.

The Titan can use **Pluck**, **Rock Throw**, or **Wing Attack** to cause you physical damage, all of which can cause decent damage. Be ready to use the most appropriate **Potion** type for healing if needed.

Once you cause over 50% damage, onto round two.

Top Tip: You can TT *twice* during Titan battles as the game auto-refills your TT ball in-between rounds. So, make sure to Terrastillize for **every round**!

Round Two

Arven shows up again and he brings along his Level 19 *Nacli* (a **Rock-type**) along to the battle.

With 2x the amount of Rocks being thrown at it, the *Bombirdier* stands **no chance** of winning.

This Titan will go down *very* quickly in round two. Two down, three to go!

Reward:

- **Surf**.

Pokémon	Level	Type	Weakness
	30		

For this battle we took our **Fire-starter** (now a Lv. 32 *Crocalor*), we also took along our trusty *Dugtrio* (with its Ground-type moves), and in back-up we had a *Pawmo*.

However, we cleared *every* round in a **single hit** by TT'ing our *Crocalor* each round and using its **Flamethrower** move.

If you don't have a **Fire-type**, then don't worry. There's *loads* of *Digletts* around the mines, so they'll do really well here too (although its *Dugtrio* evolution is a safer option).

Fighting attacks also do 2x damage as well, so there's no shortages of options here. As long as you reach this battle at Level 31 (or above), then this titan shouldn't present *too*

many issues to you as you take it on in battle. To trigger the battle, chase it around the mines until the battle starts.

Round One

It can try to hurt you with **Iron Tail** (lowering your defense), use **Wrap**, causing you damage for a few turns, or **Headbutt** (as the name implies, it's a straight-up physical attack).

You need to chase after it again to start the second round.

Round Two

Arven is of no use here, so repeat the same tactics you used in round one (TT up and hit it with your strongest attack it's weak to) and you'll find that this battle is over quicker than it takes to chase it in the first place!

Reward:

- **Jump**.

Legend Battle:
Vs. Quaking Earth Titan

Pokémon	Level	Type	Weakness
	44	Ground Fighting	Psychic Flying Grass Fairy Water

The **Scarlet-exclusive** *Great Tusk* doesn't actually have any **Ground-type** moves at its disposal.

We brought a few solid Lv. 45 Pokémon to this battle. We found our *Tinkaton* to be a very helpful as it's **Fairy-type** moves hit it hard. It also resists its **Brick Break**, **Knock Off**, and **Rapid Spin** moves.

We also took in a Lv. 46 *Gyarados* as it's both **Water** *and* **Flying** types!

Finally, we took in our strongest **Grass** (with the move **Razor Leaf**) and **Poison** Pokémon to round out our team (as *Great Tusk* is weak to poison attacks).

Round One

Great Tusk is pure physical attacks and *cannot* boost them. However, we first used our strongest Poison move on it to help chip away at its health from the beginning.

We then focused on using our strongest TT'd **Fairy** moves on it to compound the constant damage that was being caused by our Poison attack.

Round Two

Arven shows up with a Level 44 *Scovillian*. When combined, we found this opponent going down surprisingly quickly.

Reward:

- **Glide**.

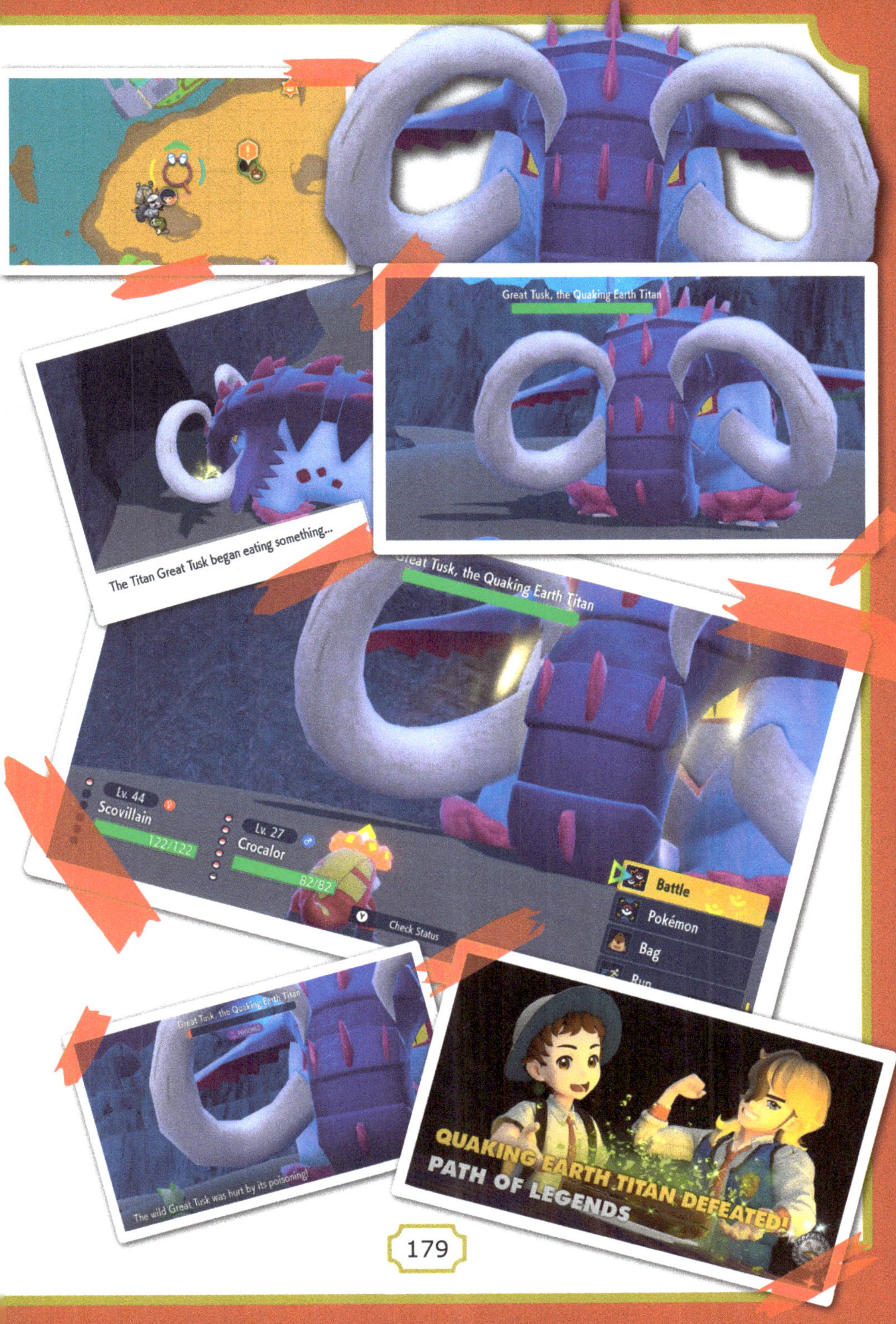

The Titan Great Tusk began eating something...

The wild Great Tusk was hurt by its poisoning!

Legend Battle: Vs. Quaking Earth Titan

Pokémon	Level	Type	Weakness
	44		

Unlike with Scarlet-exclusive *Great Tusk*, *Iron Treads* **cannot** be poisoned (but it *can* be burnt…)

We brought a few solid Lv. 45 Pokémon to this battle.

If you'd picked the **Fire-type** as your starter, then use your *Skeledirge* out for this battle.

For back-up, we took our trusty *Dugtrio* alongside it as its **Ground** moves.

Finally, we kept our Lv. 46 *Gyarados* ready for battle as it can resist a lot of *Iron Tread's* moves. Keep all **Grass-types** out of this fight as the **Fire Fang** move will burn it to shreds in seconds.

Round One

We used our hard-hitting TT'd **Flamethrower** move to deal *serious* damage to Iron Treads from the very start.

It can take a lot of punishment though, so be sure to heal up and use **Burn Heal** if needed.

Round Two

Arven's Level 44 *Scovillian* busts out the karma and uses the **Fire Fang** move back against. When combined with our kick-ass *Skeledirge*, it never really stood much of a chance,

Reward:

- **Glide**.

Iron Treads, the Quaking Earth Titan
Iron Treads, the Quaking Earth Titan
BURNED
The wild Iron Treads was burned!
QUAKING EARTH TITAN DEFEATED!
PATH OF LEGENDS

Pokémon	Level	Type	Weakness
	55		

Caution

This battle is split into two different battles with **no** chance to change your team in-between! So, make sure to prepare your final team *before* you start this fight!

For this first battle we took our Lv. 57 *Raichu*, Lv. 56 *Meowscarada*, and a Lv. 55 *Pawmot* as back-up.

For battle two, we had a Lv. 57 *Tinkaton* and a Lv. 58 *Igglypuff* ready and waiting.

We also made sure to have *plenty* of healing items to hand (these titans can hit you *hard!*).

Finally, remember to TT your strongest Pokémon at the start of each round as it automatically gets refilled between rounds.

Round One

We went in hard with our *Raichu* and it took around 3 - 4 hits (and a couple of heals) to get this battle to round two. So, be careful, and heal as needed.

Round Two

To begin round two, swim west, find a shallow area of water by a different island and you'll find the Dondozo waiting for you.

Arven jumps into the fight with his Lv. 55 *Greedent*. This Pokémon mainly uses **Normal-Type** moves (such as **Take Down**). It'll only deal 1x damage, so don't depend on it being loads of help.

Map
Path of Legends
Casseroya Lake
The Search for the False Dragon Titan
The False Dragon Titan
(Information not verified)
Titan Badge (Dragon)
Dondozo, the False Dragon
POISONED
The wild Dondozo used Water Pulse!
Lv. 55
Greedent
197/197
Lv. 49
Tinkaton
94/165
Check Status
Battle
Pokémon
Bag
Run
Dondozo, the False Dragon
The wild Dondozo used Aqua Tail!
Dondozo, the False Dragon Titan
The wild Dondozo used Aqua Tail!

Legend Battle:
Vs. False Dragon Titan (Pt. 2)

Pokémon	Level	Type	Weakness
	56		

For this battle we used the Lv. 57 *Tinkaton* and Lv. 58 *Igglypuff* for the most part, and left our remaining Part one battle Pokémon as back-ups.

We also made sure to have *plenty* of healing items to hand (as this tiny looking Titan can hit you *hard* - and leave you with lowered Accuracy - with its **Muddy Water** move).

Finally, remember to TT your strongest Pokémon at the start of each round as it gets auto-refilled between rounds.

Round One

We busted out *Igglypuff's* **Sweet Kiss** and **Disarming Voice** moves to deal maximum damage to our opponent.

If you've - bravely - brought along another **Dragon-type** along to the battle, then using Physical **Dragon** moves (such as **Breaking Swipe**, **Dragon Claw**, and **Dragon Pulse**) will offer you greater odds of winning.

Round Two

Arven jumps into the fight with his Lv. 55 *Greedent* by his side (again).

However, the False Dragon is now more likely to use status-restricting moves such as **Icy Wind** and **Taunt**, so be careful.

Reward:

- **Climb**.

Map
Path of Legends
Casseroya Lake
The Search for the False Dragon Titan
The False Dragon Titan
(Information not verified)
A highly dangerous Pokémon said to
Close
Back
Titan Badge (Dragon)
Tatsugiri, the False Dragon Titan
POISONED
The wild Tatsugiri used Taunt!
Tatsugiri, the False Dragon Titan
POISONED
The wild Tatsugiri used Muddy Water!
Tatsugiri, the False Dragon Titan
FALSE DRAGON TITAN DEFEATED
PATH OF LEGENDS

Legend Battle:
Vs. Trainer Arven

Pokémon	Level	Type	Weakness
	58		
	59		
	60		
	61		x4
	62		
	63		

Note

To trigger this battle, you must travel to the *Lighthouse* that's near *Poco Path*.

Arven has built quite the diverse collection on his travels. So, you'll need to come *well prepared* before even starting this battle!

The order Arven brings his Pokémon out depends entirely on the order *you* bring *yours* out! Cheeky! However, *Mabosstiff* is **always** his final choice.v

Your Choice of Team

Realistically, you're *really* going to want all of your Pokémon to be *at least* Level 60 (preferably Level 63), to make sure you stand the best chance.

First and foremost, you'll want your strongest **Fighting-type** as it can be used on up to four of Arven's team.

Secondly, we brought along our strongest **Flying** and **Rock-types** (our trusty *Dugtrio* with **Rock TT** proved very useful here).

Finally, a **Flying** and also a **Grass-type** Pokémon should be used to round out the remainder of your team.

None of his team are immune to **Poison**. Worth considering for early chip damage strats.

Vs. Greedent

Bring our your hardest-hitting **Fighting-type** move here. A move such as **Close Combat** has the potential to one-shot this opponent (which, is advisable, as its **Body Slam** move packs a serious punch)!

It's also worth considering TT'ing your **Fighting** Pokémon here as you'll be using it several times. Just be sure it **doesn't** faint, or you'll lose the effects!

Vs. Cloyster

If your **Fighting-type** Pokémon hasn't sustained too much damage, then use it against *Cloyster*.

Otherwise, you strongest physical **Grass** or **Rock-type** will do just as much damage (as it can use **Light Screen** to reduce damage from Sp. Attacks for up to five turns).

Vs. Scovillain

Watch out for its powerful move **Fire Blast** as it'll hit you hard (and be ready with **Burn Heal** items just in-case).

Otherwise, both **Poison** and **Rock** moves are super effective against it. So, pick your strongest of these types and go make light work of it!

Vs. Toedscruel

Bring out your strongest **Flying-type** as this opponent often uses the really powerful **Ground-type** move **Earth Power**. Otherwise, your strongest **Bug-type** will serve you well here.

Mega Potions throughout this final battle.

Keep up the hard work and you'll eventually take this Pokémon down, signaling the very end of the **Path of Legends** story-line.

Vs. Garganacl

You'll definitely want to bring your **Fighting-type** back out for this battle as it can hit you hard with both its **Stealth Rock** and **Stone Edge** moves.

Oh, and make sure you've got *plenty* of healing potions for this particular battle…

Vs. TT'd Mabosstiff

Arven's pet *Mabosstiff* is finally back to full health (thanks to your help), so it's only fitting that his old-pal gets brought out for the last fight.

While using your TT'd **Fighting-type** is the natural choice, you need to be *really* careful about its **Play Rough Fairy-type** move that hits hard (with 90% accuracy) and can lower your Attack stat too!

This is especially powerful when used against your **Fighting-type**, so be ready to use a fair few revives and

Your main traveling Pokémon is now fully powered-up, and you should be strong enough to complete the **Starfall Street** story-line (if you've not done so already).

However, if this *is* the final main game story-line now finished, there's still a *lot* more left to do…

Reward:

- **12,600 money**

Area Zero
The Way Home

Only once you've completed **all** three of the main story-line quests, will you be allowed to enter the last - very challenging - area of the game.

"Area Zero" is situated in the giant crater that's in the middle of the map. It's also home to quite a few super-powerful Pokémon, as well as special variants known as **Paradox Pokémon**.

To unlock "Area Zero", you must first receive the call from Arven who invites you to meet him there.

You can now head there either by traveling south-east from *Medali*, or by head via *Medali's* south-east exit.

Once you reach the doorway, Arven will speak with you and you must confirm you're ready to join him on this adventure.

As the - lengthy - cut-scenes progress, you'll be given the task of disabling four locks as you descend the crater.

There's *loads* of wild Pokémon wandering around as you make your way down the crater.

Prepare your team

It's critical to ensure that you have a varied team to take with you into the crater, as there's *loads* of powerful (and rare) Pokémon types waiting for you here.

If you want to save yourself from using too many healing items, then we recommend you go in with your best 6 - 10 Pokémon being all around Lv. 70+

Flying, Rock, Fairy, Ground, Dark, Electric, and Fire-types are all very solid choices for this area.

Area Zero Pokémon

You'll find the following Pokémon available to battle in Area Zero (before you reach Research Station 1). They're all *roughly* around Lv. 55, but that's not definite, so don't go in thinking they'll all be easy battles.

Pokémon	Level	Type	Weakness
	55+	Normal, Flying	Electric, Ice, Rock
	55+	Normal	Fighting
	55+	Flying, Dark	Electric, Fire
	55+	Normal, Psychic	Bug, Dark
	55+	Fairy	Poison, Steel
	55+	Ice, Bug	Fire x4, Flying, Rock x4, Steel
	55+	Normal, Psychic	Bug, Dark

Pokémon	Level	Type	Weakness
	55+		
	55+		x4
	55+		
	55+		
	55+		
	55+		
	55+		
	55+		

Feel free to battle and level-up your Pokémon as you head down the crater towards the first Research Station.

However, before you reach it, you're stopped by a completely new Pokémon, (that's exclusive to your version). So, for us, it was a Lv. 60+ *Glimmora* (Scarlet). Therefore, it'd be wise to check your party *before* you trigger the battle with it.

Pokémon	Level	Type		Weakness			
	62	⬡	👤	🟫	🔆	🧊	💧

Towards Research Base 2

Once you win the battle, enter the Research Base and press the button.

Leave, go down the hill towards Research Base 2. Let's take a look at what different Pokémon you can expect to see along the way.

Pokémon	Level	Type		Weakness				
	55+	🔥	🟫	🟫	💧 ×4			
	55+	🔆		🟢	🌑	👻		
	55+	🌿		🟢	🔥	🪶	❄️	👤
	55+	⬡		👊	🌿	🟫	🧊	💧
	55+	🔥	🟫	🟫	💧 ×4			
	55+	⚡		🟫				
	55+	⚡	👊	💗	🟫	🔆		

Once you reach the large cliff-edge, slide down the stone hill towards the base at the bottom. As you'd expect, there's *another* set Pokémon ready to battle you at the bottom.

This time, it's a variation on a classic Pokémon…

Pokémon	Level	Type	Weakness
	62		

Once the battle is over, it's time to enter the Research Lab and uncover even more of the story…

Towards Research Base 3

Pokémon	Level	Type	Weakness
	55+		x4
	55+		
	55+		
	55+		

Pokémon	Level	Type	Weakness
	55+		
	55+		x4
	55+		
	55+		
	55+		x4

Note

The green pads can be used to warp between Research Bases within the crater.

Run down the hill, under the alcove, head left, then run towards the base for your next forced battle.

Pokémon	Level	Type	Weakness
	62		

Once the battle is over, it's time to enter the Research Lab and peel back further layers of this story…

Pokémon	Level	Type	Weakness
	55+		
	55+		
	55+		
	55+		
	55+		
	55+		
	55+		

Towards Research Base 4

Once exiting the third base, down the hill, and proceed into the deep, dark cave.

Navigate your way down the winding hill until you reach the next Research Base.

Enter it, then after the cutscene, continue down the - very long and winding - hill towards the **Zero Lab**.

Pokémon	Level	Type	Weakness
	55+	Dragon / Ground	Dragon, Fairy, Ice x4
	55+	Dragon / Ground	Dragon, Fairy, Ice x4
	55+	Normal	Fighting, Grass, Ground, Rock, Water
Scarlet Only			
	55+	Dark / Dragon	Bug, Dragon, Fairy x4, Fighting, Ice
	55+	Fairy / Fire	Ghost, Ground, Steel
	55+	Dark / Dragon	Bug, Dragon, Fairy x4, Fighting, Ice
Violet Only			
	55+	Dragon / Ghost	Dark, Dragon, Fairy, Ghost, Ice
	55+	Dragon / Ghost	Dark, Dragon, Fairy, Ghost, Ice
	55+	Dark / Fighting	Electric, Fairy, Ice, Normal

Zero Lab

Once you reach the lab at the bottom of the crystal-packed crater, it's time for a rally of battles against a number of powerful *Paradox Pokémon*.

Let's take a look at each one (however, the order in which *you* face them may be different). So, be sure to refer back to this list for their types and weakness(es).

Pokémon	Level	Type	Weakness
Scarlet Only			
	64	Ground / Fighting	Fairy, Flying, Grass, Ice, Psychic, Water
	64	Grass / Dark	Bug x4, Fighting, Fire, Flying, Ice, Ground
	64	Ghost / Fairy	Ghost, Steel
Violet Only			
	64	Ice / Water	Electric, Fighting, Grass, Rock
	64	Dark / Flying	Electric, Fairy, Ice, Rock
	64	Fighting / Electric	Ground, Fairy, Psychic

As soon as you've beaten the three Paradox Pokémon that attacked you, it's time for you to enter Zero Lab and unveil some unexpected plot twists…

The Way Home
Vs. AI Sada (Scarlet)

Pokémon	Level	Type	Weakness
	66	Grass / Fighting	Psychic, Fire, Flying, x4 Fairy
	66	Fairy / Normal	Ghost, Fighting, Steel
	66	Grass / Dark	x4 Bug, Psychic, Fighting, Fire, Flying, Ice, Fairy
	66	Ghost / Fairy	Ghost, Steel
	66	Electric / Ground	Grass, Ground, Ice, Water
	67	Dark / Dragon	x4 Bug, Dragon, Fairy, Fighting, Ice

The game warns you that you'll have to battle the AI *before* you initiate the battle. This gives you plenty of time to read up on what you're up against.

Your Choice of Team

Make sure you're leading with a team (ideally around Lv. 70+), we used the following:

Tinkaton (Fairy/Steel):

- *Scream Tail,*
- *Flutter Mane,*
- *Roaring Moon,*
- *Slither Wing (Back-up).*

Corviknight (Flying/Steel):

- *Slither Wing,*
- *Brute Bonnet (Back-up),*
- *Scream Tail (Back-up),*
- *Flutter Mane (Back-up).*

Frostmoth (Ice/Bug):

- *Brute Bonnet,*
- *Sandy Shocks,*
- *Roaring Moon (Back-up).*

Notable Alternatives:

- *Glimmora (Rock/Poison),*
- *Scream Tail (Fairy/Psychic),*
- *Dugtrio (Ground/Steel).*

Vs. Slither Wing

Clearly, use your **Flying-type** here (4x damage). Be careful of its varied attacks. **Leech Life** drains your HP, giving it to them, **Low Sweep** hits **Steel-types** hard, it can also use **Zen Headbutt** (for Flinch), and **Lunge**.

Vs. Scream Tail

Be *very* wary of its **Drain Punch** move on **Steel-types**, as it's Super Effective (while also restoring their own health)! Cheeky! Be ready to revive any Steel-types you have (just in-case its faster than you).

Vs. Brute Bonnet

It's **Bug-type** all the way here (4x damage). Make sure to hit first as it can use **Giga Drain**, **Sucker Punch, Payback,** or **Earth Power** to hit you hard.

Vs. Flutter Mane

We used **Light Screen** to help protects us from Flutter's **Shadow Ball** Sp. Att.

Also be wary of its **Mystical Fire** (strong against **Steel-types**), **Power Gem**, and **Thunderbolt**. Ouch!

Vs. Sandy Shocks

This Pokémon brings **Earth Power, Power Gem, Discharge,** and **Flash Cannon** to the party. We used our **Ice-type** here (with our *Dugtrio* for back-up).

Vs. Roaring Moon

Fairy-types excel in this final battle (dealing both 4x damage *and* resisting its STAB moves!).

Just make sure it doesn't hit you with its **Stone Edge, Earthquake,** or **Dragon Claw** moves that is…

Congratulations! You've finally did it! Or… have you? (Answer: No).

The FINAL Challenge!

This is it. The final challenge in the main story-line has arrived. This has been the culmination of everything you've worked hard for. And… you can't even use **any** of the Pokémon you've worked hard to catch!

OK. So, when you're given the chance to go into your Menu, select the very bottom option.

That's right! You can now, finally, use the *Koraidon* that's been with you the whole time! Sweet!

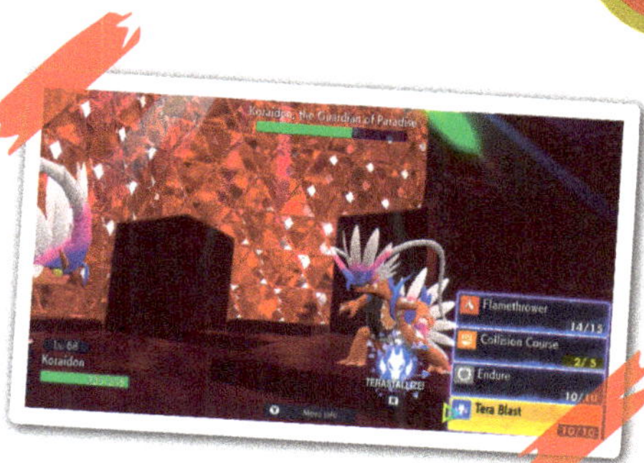

The main strategy here is to focus on using **Collision Course** as it deals the most damage.

However, the opposing *Koraidon* will happily use moves such as **Flamethrower**, **Endure, Giga Impact, Taunt,** and **Bulk Up** to wear you down.

Make sure to use as many **Full Restores** or **Max Potions** as required to keep you in the fight.

Once you can TT, do so, and use **Tera Blast** to finish this fight once and for all!

CONGRATULATIONS!
You did it! Well done!

Enjoy the cut-scene, then it's time to do the post-game…

The Way Home
Vs. AI Turo (Violet)

Pokémon	Level	Type	Weakness
	66	Fire / Psychic	Ground x4, Fairy, Ghost, Water
	66	Ice / Water	Electric, Fighting, Grass, Ghost
	66	Fighting / Electric	Ground, Psychic, Fairy
	66	Dark / Flying	Electric, Fairy, Ice, Ghost
	66	Ghost / Electric	Fighting, Grass, Ground x4, Water
	67	Fairy / Fighting	Fairy, Flying, Psychic, Steel, Poison

The game warns you that you'll have to battle the AI *before* you initiate the battle. This gives you plenty of time to read up on what you're up against.

Your Choice of Team

Make sure you're leading with a team (ideally around Lv. 70+), we used the following:

Dugtrio (Ground/Steel):

Ours had **Rock-TT** moves.

- *Iron Moth,*
- *Iron Hands,*
- *Iron Thorns,*
- *Iron Jugulis (Back-up).*

Raichu (Electric):

- *Iron Bundle,*
- *Iron Jugulis.*

Girafarig (Normal/Psychic):

- *Iron Valiant,*
- *Iron Moth (Back-up),*
- *Iron Hands (Back-up).*

Notable Alternatives:

- *Glimmora (Rock/Poison),*
- *Corviknight (Flying/Steel).*
- *Tinkaton (Trade) (Fairy/Steel)*

Vs. Iron Moth

Clearly, use your **Ground-type** here (4x damage). Be careful of its varied attacks. It has access to: **Air Slash, Fiery Dance, Discharge,** and **Sludge Wave**.

Vs. Iron Bundle

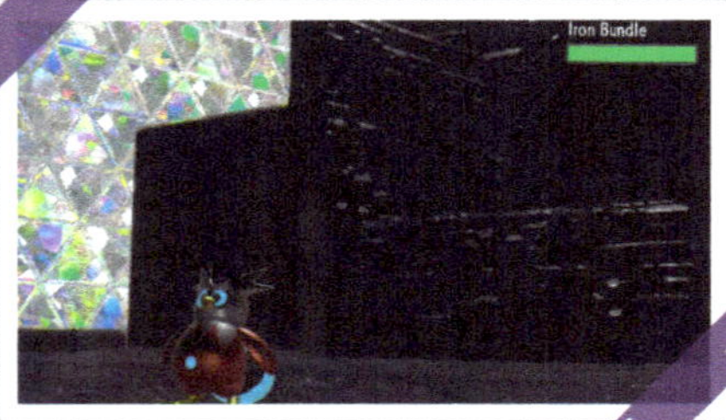

Use an **Electric-type** here to speed this battle up. It can use: **Snowscape, Freeze-Dry, Drill Peck,** and **Water Pulse** to wear you down.

Vs. Iron Hands

A **Ground-Type** here works well. Watch out for it using any of the following: **Iron Head, Drain Punch, Fake Out,** and **Thunder Punch.**

Vs. Iron Jugulis

Use your **Electric-Type** again. Be careful of it using the following moves: **Flamethrower, Dark Pulse, Flash Cannon,** and **Air Slash** (STAB).

Vs. Iron Thorns

Ground-types deal 4x damage! Thanks *Dugtrio*! Move wise, watch out for: **Earthquake, Stone Edge, Brick Break,** and **Thunder Punch** (STAB).

Vs. Iron Valiant

Fairy-types excel in this final battle. Watch out for it using: **Poison Jab, Brick Break** (Fighting STAB)**, Spirit Break** (Fairy STAB)**,** and **Psycho Cut.**

Just make sure it doesn't hit you with its **Stone Edge, Earthquake,** or **Dragon Claw** moves that is…

Congratulations! You've finally did it! Or… have you? (Answer: No).

The FINAL Challenge!

This is it. The final challenge in the main story-line has arrived. This has been the culmination of everything you've worked hard for. And… you can't even use **any** of the Pokémon you've worked hard to catch!

OK. So, when you're given the chance to go into your Menu, select the very bottom option.

That's right! You can now, finally, use the *Miraidon* that's been with you the whole time! Sweet!

The main strategy here is to focus on using **Power Gem** or **Tera Blast** as they deal the most damage - for now.

However, the opposing *Miraidon* will happily use moves such as **Hyper Beam**, **Charge**, **Power Gem**, **Taunt**, and **Endure** to wear you down.

Make sure to use as many **Full Restores** or **Max Potions** as required to keep you in the fight.

Once you can TT, do so, and use **Tera Blast** to finish this fight once and for all!

CONGRATULATIONS!
You did it! Well done!

Enjoy the cut-scene, then it's time to do the post-game…

Ruined Four
Hidden Legendary Pokémon

There's an additional set of Legendary Pokémon that can be fought (and caught). However, to unlock these, you must locate **32** colored stakes that are stuck into the ground.

Each stake glows a specific color and you must find all **eight** stakes *of each color* to unlock the shrine that houses one of the four Ruined Legendary Pokémon.

Those colors are: *Blue, Green, Orange, Purple.*

The game purposefully doesn't track (or reveal) any information on the quest to find these hidden stakes, or any of these four Legendary Pokémon (at least, not until you finish "The Way Home"). Therefore, to make your life easier we suggest that you:

1. *Focus on collecting every stake for one color at a time.*

2. *Use our exclusive "Collected?" tick box to keep a track of the ones you've pulled out so far.*

Caution

We **strongly** recommend that you bring a Pokémon knows the move **False Swipe** for *every* Legendary Pokémon as that prevents you from accidentally knocking it out (which, can be done easily by accident - *especially* if it's 4x weak to a type).

Finally, as they're all *really* hard to catch, use a status-ailment (such as **Paralyze**), and - ideally - use a **Dusk Ball** to catch them.

Ruined Four
Blue Stakes (Chi-Yu)

Blue Stake No. 1

Use Climb or Glide to head up the hill north of the *Area One* (*North Province*).

Blue Stake No. 2

Found on the cliff, northeast of *Area Two, North Province's* Pokémon Center.

Blue Stake No. 3

Found near a tree close to the right-hand border of the snowy *Glaseado Mountain*.

Blue Stake No. 4

Look for a lonesome patch of grass on top of the mountain near the *Poison Crew*. Can be found near a tree up here.

Blue Stake No. 5

Look for a bent tree that overlooks the *Tagtree Thicket*. waterfall, the stake is here.

Blue Stake No. 6

Hiding behind a tree that's located on top of a plateau, northwest of the *Lighthouse* in *Levincia*.

Blue Stake No. 7

Travel southeast from *Fury Falls* and there's some ruins near the sea. The stake is located in the far corner, under the roof.

Blue Stake No. 8

Climb to the top of Fury Falls (located in *Area Two, North Province*). The stake is in the grass up here.

The Blue Shrine Gate

Head inside the waterfall cave at the top of *Fury Falls*, and approach the shrine to start the battle.

Collected?
1
Collected?
2
Collected?
3
4
Collected?

5
Collected?
6
Collected?
7
8
Collected?
Collected?

Pokémon	Level	Type	Weakness
	60		

It's critical to know that *Chi-Yu* excels with its very high Sp. Att and Sp. Def stats.

It can also use a range of harsh attacks. **Ruination** halves your HP, its **Beads of Ruin** move lowers your Sp. Def at the very beginning too.

Its attack **Lava Plume** uses **Fire** STAB (causing **Burn**) and **Swagger** confuses your Pokémon (while also boosting its Attack stat by *two* levels)!

The good news is, is that it *can't* regenerate its own health.

It's worth giving your key Pokémon an **X Sp. Def** item to hold as well.

Ideally, use a **Fire-type** (immune to **Burn**) and *a lot* of healing items, or a **Rock-type** (and *a lot* of healing items!).

Watch out for Chi-Yu using **Bounce** to evade your Poké balls. Sending it to Sleep can help (along with a **Dream Ball**).

Ultimately, be ready to heal (loads), chip away at its health (so NO 100+ attacks!), and bring a load of Poké balls.

Ruined Four

Green Stakes (Ting-Lu)

Green Stake No. 1

From *Porto Marinada (West Province, Area Two)*, go east to *Colonnade Hollow*. Look inside the cave, on top of a pillar.

Green Stake No. 2

Located in the open grass, north of Stake No. 1 (just before the bridge that leads to *Casseroya Lake*).

Green Stake No. 3

Located on a small hill that overlooks the southwest corner of *Casseroya Lake*.

Green Stake No. 4

Tucked away on the smallest island to the south of *Casseroya Lake*.

Green Stake No. 5

Go to the middle of the hill on the western side of the largest island on *Casseroya Lake*.

Green Stake No. 6

On a mound of dirt, close to the sea, northwest of *Casseroya Lake*.

Green Stake No. 7

Found at the bottom of the mountain (directly west of the ice gym), behind a rock, near the river.

Green Stake No. 8

Look for where *Glaseado Mountain* and *Casseroya Lake* meet (northwest corner of the map). Located on a cliff right at the edge, near the sea.

The Green Shrine Gate

Head to the middle of the mountains (located west of Stake No. 8) and walk up the long path to the Green Shrine.

1
Collected?
2
Collected?
3
Collected?
4
Collected?

5
Collected?
6
Collected?
7
Collected?
8
Collected?

Pokémon	Level	Type	Weakness

| | 60 | | |

It's critical to know that *Ting-Lu* excels with its very high Defense and HP, solid Attack and Sp. Def stats, but has lower Speed and Sp. Att stats.

It can also use a range of harsh attacks. **Ruination** halves your HP, its **Vessel of Ruin** move lowers your Sp. Att at the very beginning too, and **Rock Slide** to hit flying Pokémon.

Its attack **Stomping Tantrum** uses **Ground** STAB and **Throat Chop** for both Dark STAB, while disabling sound-based attacks.

On the plus side it *can't* regenerate its own health.

It's worth giving your key Pokémon an **X Defense** item to hold as well.

Ideally, use a Pokémon such as *Hawlucha* as it only takes 1x damage from **Rock Slide** (while dodging its **Stomping Ground** attack). It can also learn **False Swipe** if required.

Ultimately, be ready to heal (loads), chip away at its health (so NO 100+ attacks!), and bring a load of Poké balls.

Ruined Four
Orange Stakes (Chien-Pao)

Orange Stake No. 1

Go to *Area Six* of *South Province*, and head up the tall cliff that overlooks the river heading into the sea.

Orange Stake No. 2

Go to the clifftops that are situated northeast from *Alfornada*. The Stake is on a patch of grass up here.

Orange Stake No. 3

Head slightly north from Stake No. 2 and go inside the middle of the hidden cave entrance, found just off the corner of this winding path.

Orange Stake No. 4

Continue north from Stake No. 3. This one is tucked away high up on a cliff. Use Climb to reach it more easily.

Orange Stake No. 5

Sitting by a tree right behind the *Water Gym*. Simple as that.

Orange Stake No. 6

Look for the ruins close to the Watchtower in *West Province, Area One*. Turn east and the Stake overlooks the ruins.

Orange Stake No. 7

Go east from Stake No.6, climb up the cliffs, and look for the stake sneakily tucked away by the nook, in the top corner.

Orange Stake No. 8

From the *West Province (Area One)* Pokémon Center, go northwest and head up the hill near the bridge. Go inside the crater for this Stake.

The Orange Shrine Gate

From Stake No. 8, it's located northwest towards the clifftop (and directly west of the round pool of water on the map).

Collected?
1
2
Collected?
Collected?
3
4
Collected?

5
Collected?
6
Collected?
7
Collected?
8
Collected?

Pokémon	Level	Type	Weakness
	60	☽ ❄	🦠 🦋 👊 *x4* 🔥 ⚪ 🪨

It's critical to know that *Chien-Pao* excels with its very high Speed and Attack stats.

It can also use a range of harsh attacks. **Ruination** halves your HP, its **Sword of Ruin** move lowers your Def at the very beginning too.

Its attack **Icicle Crash** uses Ice STAB (causing flinch) and **Sacred Sword** to deal Fighting-type damage. **Sucker Punch** can allow it to hit you first (if you try an use an attacking move on it).

The good news is, is that it *can't* regenerate its own health.

It's worth giving your key Pokémon an **X Sp. Def** item to hold as well.

Ideally, DON'T use a **Fighting-type** (too easy to KO it with 4x damage). Instead, chip away with less-powerful moves and heal often as it hits hard.

As with all of the Ruined Pokemon, make sure you bring plenty of Poké Balls if you want to catch it and add it to your Pokédex permanently.

Ruined Four
Purple Stakes (Wo-Chien)

Purple Stake No. 1

Go southwest from the *Los Platos* Pokémon Center and head to the pool of water. The stake is up on a hill that overlooks the town.

Purple Stake No. 2

This time, go northeast from the same *Los Platos* Pokémon Center. You'll find this stake on a hill that overlooks *Mesagoza City*.

Purple Stake No. 3

Head to the spiral hilltop that's on the map. The next stake is waiting at the top.

Purple Stake No. 4

It's on the hill that overlooks the bridge (overlooking *South Province, Area Three*) located slightly northwest of the spiral hill.

Purple Stake No. 5

Go west, from the *South Province, Area Three* Pokémon Center, and along the top of the cliffs. The stake is overlooking the city.

Purple Stake No. 6

After unlocking the *Watchtower* (located in *South Province, Area Three*), go north to the top of these canyons to find the stake.

Purple Stake No. 7

On a hill that *directly overlooks* the *Artazon* Pokémon Center.

Purple Stake No. 8

Go to the ruins by the sea of *South Province, Area Five*. Face the sea, then look up and left, towards the hill for the stake.

The Purple Shrine Gate

Drop down off the hill to find the Shrine Gate. Easy!

Collected?
2
Collected?
3
Collected?
4
Collected?

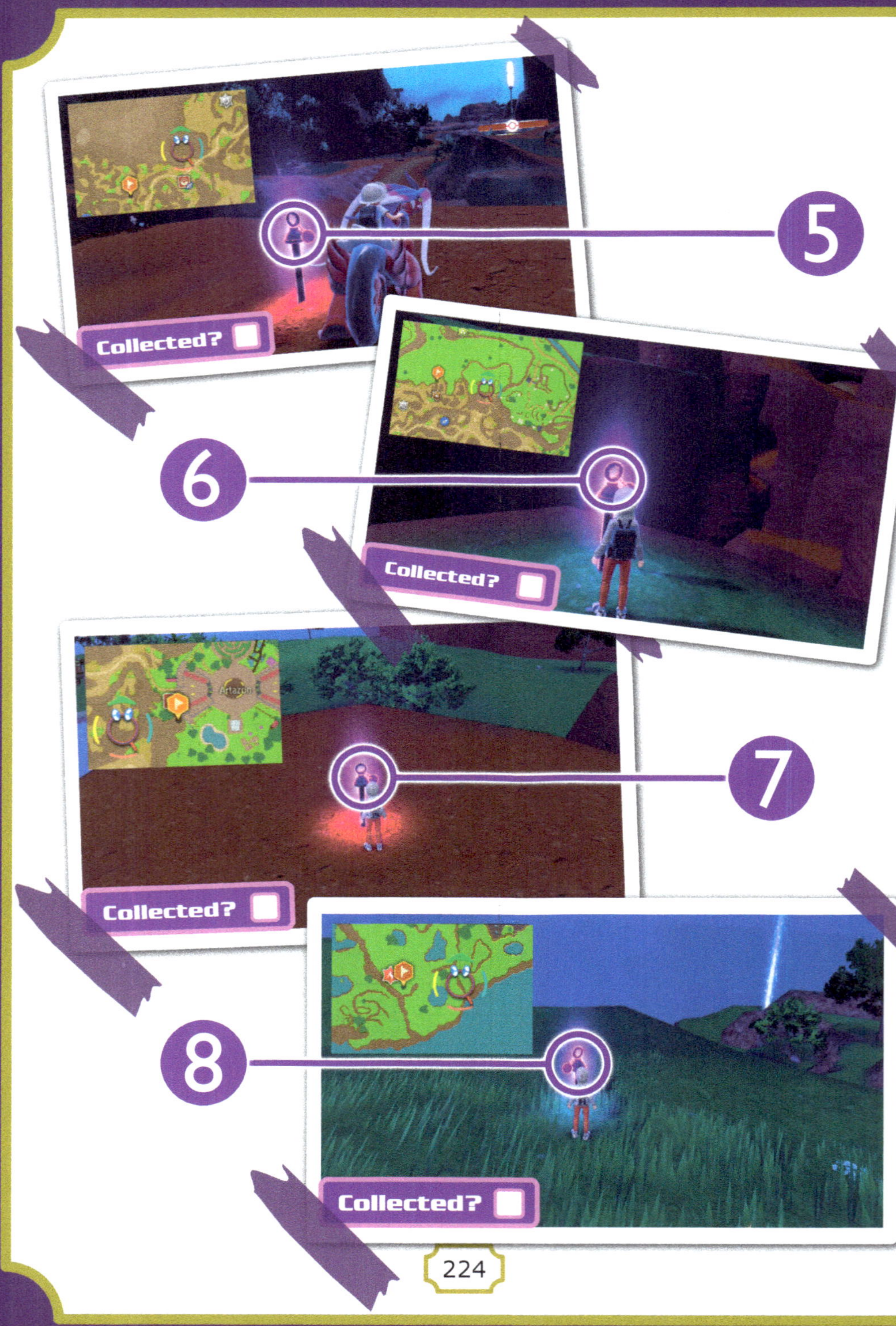

5
Collected?
6
Collected?
7
Artazon
Collected?
8
Collected?

Pokémon	Level	Type	Weakness
	60	⚫🟢	🟢 x4 🎀 🪶 ✊ 🔥 ❄ 🟣

It's critical to know that *Wo-Chien* excels with its very high Sp. Def, Defense (but slow Speed because, well, it's a snail).

It can also use a range of harsh attacks. **Ruination** halves your HP, its **Tablets of Ruin** move lowers your Attack at the very beginning too.

Its attack **Giga Drain and Power Whip** uses **Grass** STAB and **Foul Play** to turn your Pokémon's attack power against it. **Giga Drain** also restores its health (by the same amount it damages you by).

It's worth giving your key Pokémon an **X Sp. Def** item to hold as well (to reduce how much health it can regenerate with **Giga Drain**).

Ideally, *DON'T* use a **Bug-type** (too easy to KO it with 4x damage). Instead, chip away with less-powerful moves and heal often as it hits hard.

As with all of the Ruined Pokemon, make sure you bring plenty of Poké Balls if you want to catch it and add it to your Pokédex permanently (but you'll most likely need to inflict a status ailment first).

Once you've beaten the main story-line and watched the end credits, then there's still a lot more on offer.

So, let's take a quick look at some of the quests you can choose to take on:

Gym Inspection Task

Head back to the Director's Office at your university and Geeta will ask you to re-visit each Gym to inspect them.

However, rather than just taking a look for any dust or litter, you're given a chance to battle them again. Only, this time, with Pokémon that are all Lv. 65+!

The key thing to keep in mind here is that the early-level gyms now have fully-evolved Pokémon to fight (opening up dual-type fights and access to more powerful moves).

Academy Ace Tournament

Once you've won every rematch against the gym leaders, report back to *Geeta* and answer her little quick to be rewarded with a **King's Rock**. Sweet!

Go to your bed, sleep wake up (a *week* later!) and then head to the *Entrance Hall*. Speak with *Nemona* again and then chat with the person standing at the side of the reception desk to kick-start this new challenge off.

Note

This challenge consists of four rounds and is a *single-elimination* style battle. You cannot leave until the battle's over, there's also zero breaks (but your team are fully healed between battles).

Your first four opponents are:

Arven, Jacq, Dendra, and *Geeta*

Each subsequent attempt
after winning this one is
against a random pool of
University staff (and *Arven*),
up to round four at least.

Round four consists of:

Clavell, *Hassel*, *Geeta*, and
Nemona.

Your reward is a special
cap for the first win, and
then it's a random item
for each tournament
that you win after.

You can retry this
as many times as you
wish.

Item Tables

For you data-fans out there...

We close out our guide with the reference part. Over the next 50+ pages, you'll find hand-crafted tables that we've spent a *lot* of time preparing and making sure they're as accurate as they can be (at the time of writing in Jan' 2023).

We've tried to be as thorough as we can and we hope you find the tables helpful and easy-to-use.

Our comprehensive tables cover the following items:

Item Type	Page No
Berries	232
Poké Balls	237
Key Items	240
Treasures	241
Battle Items	242
Held Battle Items	244
Vitamins and Feathers	252
Medicine	253
Type-specific TMs	256 - 276
Tera Shards	277
Evolution Items	279
Sandwich Fillings	283

Berries

Item Name	Icon	Description	Location(s)
Aguav Berry		Restores up to half of max HP.	Sparkling Item, Tera Raids
Apicot Berry		Increases Sp. Def by one.	Sparkling Item, Tera Raids
Aspear Berry		Cures frostbite.	ES Practice, Tera Raids
Babiri Berry		Reduces super-effective Steel moves by 50%.	Sparkling Item, Tera Raids
Charti Berry		Reduces super-effective Rock moves by 50%	Sparkling Item
Cheri Berry		Cures paralysis.	ES Practice, Sparkling Item, Tera Raids
Chesto Berry		Cures drowsiness.	Sparkling Item, Tera Raids
Chilian Berry		Reduces super-effective Normal moves by 50%	Sparkling Item, Tera Raids
Chople Berry		Reduces effect from effective Fighting moves.	Sparkling Item, Tera Raids
Coba Berry		educes super-effective Flying moves by 50%	Sparkling Item, Tera Raids

Item Name	Icon	Description	Location(s)
Colbur Berry		Reduces super-effective Dark moves by 50%	Sparkling Item, Tera Raids
Figy Berry		Restores up to half of max HP. Causes confusion if user hates it.	ES Practice, Sparkling Item, Tera Raids
Ganlon Berry		Increases Def by one.	ES Practice, Sparkling Item, Tera Raids
Grepa Berry		Pokémon grows friendly, but loses base Sp. Def stat.	Alfornada, Porto Marinada, E.Province A1, Tera Raids
Haban Berry		Reduces super-effective Dragon moves by 50%	Sparkling Item, Tera Raids
Hondew Berry		Increases friendliness, while lowering Sp. Atk stat.	Alfornada, Porto Marinada, Tera Raids
Lapapa Berry		Restores HP, but causes confuse if not liked.	Alfornada, Dalizapa Passage, West Province Area Two, Tera Raids
Kasib Berry		Reduces super-effective Ghost moves by 50%	Sparkling Item, Tera Raids

Item Name	Icon	Description	Location(s)
Kebia Berry		Reduces super-effective Poison moves by 50%	Sparkling Item, Tera Raids
Kelpsy Berry		Increases friendliness, while lowering base Atk stat.	Alfornada, Porto Marinada, Star Tera Raid Battles
Leppa Berry		Restores 10 PP to a move.	ES Practice, Tera Raids
Liechi Berry		Boost Att by one stage.	ES Practice, Sparkling Item, Tera Raids
Lum Berry		Cures any status ailments.	ES Practice, Sparkling Item, Tera Raids
Mago Berry		Restores up to half of max HP. Causes confusion if user hates it.	ES Practice, Sparkling Item, Tera Raids
Micle Berry		Boosts Accuracy by one stage.	Sparkling Item, Tera Raids
Occa Berry		Reduces super-effective Fire moves by 50%	Sparkling Item, Tera Raids
Oran Berry		Restores up to 10HP.	ES Practice, Sparkling Item, Tera Raids
Passho Berry		Reduces super-effective Water moves by 50%	Sparkling Item, Tera Raids

Item Name	Icon	Description	Location(s)
Payapa Berry		Reduces super-effective Psychic moves by 50%	Sparkling Item, Tera Raids
Pecha Berry		Cures poisoning.	ES Practice, Sparkling Item, Tera Raids
Persim Berry		Cures confusion.	ES Practice, Sparkling Item, Tera Raids
Pomeg		Pokémon grows friendly, loses base HP stat.	Alfornada, Porto Marinada
Qualot		Pokémon grows friendly, loses base Def stat.	Alfornada, Porto Marinada, E. Province A1
Rawst Berry		Cures burn.	Sparkling Item, Tera Raids
Rindo Berry		Reduces super-effective Grass moves by 50%	Sparkling Item, Tera Raids
Roseli Berry		Reduces super-effective Fairy moves by 50%	Sparkling Item, Tera Raids
Salac Berry		Boosts Speed stat by one stage.	Sparkling Item, Tera Raids
Shuca Berry		Reduces super-effective Ground moves by 50%	Sparkling Item, Tera Raids
Sitrus Berry		Restores a small amount of HP.	Sparkling Item, Tera Raids

Item Name	Icon	Description	Location(s)
Starf Berry		Boosts a random stat by one stage.	Sparkling Item, Tera Raids
Tamato Berry		Pokémon grows friendly, loses base Speed stat.	Alfornada, E.Province A1, Porto Marinada, Tera Raids
Tanga Berry		Reduces super-effective Bug moves by 50%	Sparkling Item, Tera Raids
Wacan Berry		Reduces super-effective Electric moves by 50%	Sparkling Item, Tera Raids
Wiki Berry		Restores up to half of max HP. Causes confusion if user hates it.	ES Practice, Tera Raids
Yache Berry		Reduces super-effective Ice moves by 50%	Sparkling Item, Tera Raids

Poké Balls

Item Name	Icon	Description	Location(s)
Cherish Ball		Used to hold Pokémon given away in events.	Special Events
Dive Ball		Best used to catch Pokémon in (or on) the water.	Porto Marinada (Auction)
Dream Ball		Use on sleeping Pokémon.	Porto Marinada (Auction)
Dusk Ball		Use to catch Pokémon in dark areas/ night time.	E.Province (A3) Porto Marinada (Auction)
Fast Ball		Use on Pokémon that are quick to run away from you.	Porto Marinada (Auction)
Friend Ball		Wild Pokémon are more friendly to you.	Porto Marinada (Auction)
Great Ball		Higher catch-rate over Poké Ball (1.5x).	Levincia Porto Marinada (Auction)
Heal Ball		Restores HP and removes status ailments	Area Zero Porto Marinada (Auction)

Item Name	Icon	Description	Location(s)
Heavy Ball		Heavier = more effective.	Porto Marinada (Auction)
Level Ball		More effective when capturing Pokémon of a lower level to your team.	Porto Marinada (Auction)
Love Ball		Most effective when target is of opposite gender.	Porto Marinada (Auction)
Lure Ball		Best Used when catching in, or on water.	Porto Marinada (Auction)
Luxury Ball		Pokémon become friendlier when caught in one.	Levincia Porto Marinada (Auction)
Master Ball		Guaranteed catch. Very rare!	Naranja & Uva Academies
Moon Ball		Use on Pokémon that can evolve using a *Moon Stone*.	Porto Marinada (Auction)
Nest Ball		Most effective on lower-level targets.	Porto Marinada (Auction)

Item Name	Icon	Description	Location(s)
Net Ball		Best used on Water and Bug-types.	Porto Marinada (Auction)
Park Ball		Used in Pal Park only.	Pal Park
Poké Ball		The standard ball for catching Pokémon in.	Most places!
Premier Ball		Same as a Poké Ball.	Porto Marinada (Auction)
Quick Ball		Higher catch rate at start of an encounter.	Levincia Porto Marinada (Auction)
Repeat Ball		Higher catch rate with pre-caught Pokémon. (3x).	Porto Marinada (Auction)
Safari Ball		1.5x rate when used in a Safari Zone.	Safari Zones (Kanto and Sinnoh regions)
Sport Ball		1.5x rate when it was used in a Bug Capture Contest only.	Johto region.
Timer Ball		More turns in battle = higher catch rate.	Area Zero Porto Marinada (Auction)
Ultra Ball		2x capture rate.	Levincia Porto Marinada (Auction) Naranja & Uva Academies

Key Items

Item Name	Icon	Description	Location(s)
Adventure Guide		Retains the advice given during the game.	Cabo Poco
Kofu's Wallet		Return it to the leader of the Cascarrafa Gym.	Cascarrafa
Koraidon's Poké Ball		Holds Koraidon	Poco Path
Miraidon's Poké Ball		Holds Miraidon	Poco Path
Rotom Catalog		A catalog of devices that Rotom likes.	Porto Marinada (auction) Requires Rotom Phone first.
Rotom Phone		Run lots of different apps.	Cabo Poco
Shiny Charm		Increase odds of finding a Shiny Pokémon.	Complete the Pokédex.
Tera Orb		Use to terastallize Pokémon.	Mesagoza

Treasures

Item Name	Icon	Description
Balm Mushroom		Sell at shops.
Big Bamboo Shoot		Sell at shops.
Comet Shard		Sell at shops.
Nugget		Sell at shops.
Pearl		Sell at shops.
Pretty Feather		Sell at shops.
Rare Bone		Sell at shops.
Star Piece		Sell at shops.
Stardust		Sell at shops.
Tiny Bamboo		Sell at shops.
Tiny Mushroom		Sell at shops.

 Battle Items

Item Name	Icon	Description	Location(s)
Dire Hit		Boosts critical hit odds once. Wears off if Pokémon leaves battle.	Chansey Supply
Guard Spec		Prevents stat reduction for five turns for all in the party.	Chansey Supply
Poké Doll		Guarantees escape from wild battles.	Poké Marts, via Pickup Ability.
X Attack		Boosts attack stats once. Wears off if the Pokémon leaves the battle.	Chansey Supply
X Defense		Boosts defense stats once. Wears off if the Pokémon leaves the battle.	Chansey Supply, Poco Path
X Sp. Atk		Boosts Sp. Atk stats once. Wears off if the Pokémon leaves the battle.	Chansey Supply
X Sp. Def		Boosts Sp. Def stats once. Wears off if the Pokémon leaves the battle.	Chansey Supply
X Speed		Boosts Speed stats once. Wears off if the Pokémon leaves the battle.	Chansey Supply

Item Name	Icon	Description	Location(s)
X Accuracy		Boosts accuracy stats once. Wears off if the Pokémon leaves the battle.	Chansey Supply

Held Battle Items

Item Name	Icon	Description	Location/Cost
Ability Shield		Prevents holder's ability from being changed.	Mesagoza Costs: 20,000
Absorb Bulb		Boosts Sp. Atk stat once if hit with a Water-type attack.	Cascarrafa Costs: 5,000
Adrenaline Orb		Boosts speed if intimidated.	Levincia Costs: 5,000
Air Balloon		Increases chance of a missed attack.	Cascarrafa Costs: 15,000
Assault Vest		Raises Sp. Def stat, but can no longer use status moves.	Mesagoza Costs: 50,000
Big Root		Boosts HP recovered from HP-stealing moves.	Cascarrafa Costs: 10,000
Binding Band		Boosts power of binding moves.	Levincia Costs: 20,000
Black Belt		Boosts Fighting-types moves.	Levincia Costs: 3,000
Black Glasses		Boosts Dark-type moves.	Levincia Costs: 3,000
Black Sludge		Restores HP to Poison-type Pokémon, hurts all others.	Levincia Costs: 10,000

Item Name	Icon	Description	Location/Cost
Blunder Policy		Raises Speed stat, if a move is missed.	Mesagoza Costs: 30,000
Cell Battery		Boosts Electric-type moves.	Cascarrafa Costs: 5,000
Charcoal		Boosts Fire-type moves.	Mesagoza Costs: 3,000
Choice Band		Boosts Attack, but only allows one move.	Mesagoza Costs: 100,000
Choice Scarf		Boosts Speed, but only allows one move.	Mesagoza Costs: 100,000
Choice Specs		Boosts Sp. Att, but only allows one move.	Mesagoza Costs: 100,000
Covert Cloak		Protects from the effects of some moves.	Levincia Costs: 20,000
Clear Amulet		Prevents to stats being lowered.	Mesagoza Costs: 30,000
Damp Rock		Extends the duration of *Rain Dance* move.	Cascarrafa Costs: 8,000
Destiny Knot		User becomes infatuated.	Mesagoza Costs: 20,000
Dragon Fang		Boosts Dragon-type moves.	Cascarrafa Costs: 3,000
Eject Button		Auto-switch out when hit.	Levincia Costs: 30,000
Eject Pack		Switch out if stats become lowered.	Levincia Costs: 30,000

Item Name	Icon	Description	Location/Cost
Electric Seed		Boosts Def on Electric terrain.	*Cascarrafa* Costs: 20,000
Eviolite		Boosts Def and Sp. Def by 50% (if the user can evolve).	*Mesagoza* Costs: 50,000
Expert Belt		Boosts super-effective moves.	*Mesagoza* Costs: 30,000
Flame Orb		Afflicts the holder with Burn status.	*Levincia* Costs: 15,000
Float Stone		Reduces weight of the holder when using a weight-based attack.	*South Province Area Five*
Focus Band		Prevents KO, by leaving 1 HP.	*Mesagoza* Costs: 10,000
Focus Sash		If you have full HP, prevents KO, by leaving 1 HP.	*Mesagoza* Costs: 50,000
Grassy Seed		Boosts Def on grassy terrain.	*Cascarrafa* Costs: 20,000
Grip Claw		Extends the duration of multi-turn attacks.	*Mesagoza* Costs: 10,000
Hard Stone		Boosts Rock-type moves.	*Cascarrafa* Costs: 3,000
Heat Rock		Extends the duration of the move *Sunny Day*	*Cascarrafa* Costs: 8,000
Heavy-Duty Boots		Prevents traps from working.	*Levincia* Costs: 20,000

Item Name	Icon	Description	Location/Cost
Icy Rock		Extends the duration of the move *Hail*.	*Cascarrafa* Costs: 8,000
Iron Ball		Lowers Speed, also allows Ground-types to hit Flying-types.	*Levincia* Costs: 20,000
King's Rock		Increases target's chance of flinching by 10%	Mesagoza Costs: 10,000
Lagging Tail		Greatly reduces your Speed.	*Levincia* Costs: 20,000
Leftovers		Slowly restores HP in battle.	*Cascarrafa* Costs: 20,000
Life Orb		Boosts damage, but costs some HP per hit.	*Mesagoza* Costs: 50,000
Light Ball		Boosts *Pikachu's* Att and Sp. Att.	5% Chance on a *Wild Pikachu*
Light Clay		Protective moves last longer.	*Cascarrafa* Costs: 20,000
Loaded Dice		Ensures multi-hit strikes hit more often.	Levincia Costs: 20,000
Luminous Moss		Boosts Sp. Def if hit by Water-type attack.	*Cascarrafa* Costs: 5,000
Magnet		Boosts Electric-type moves.	Cascarrafa Costs: 3,000
Mental Herb		Removes move-binding effects.	*Cascarrafa* Costs: 10,000

Item Name	Icon	Description	Location/Cost
Metal Coat		Boosts Steel-type moves.	*Levincia* Costs: 3,000
Metronome		Boosts consecutive moves, until the move used is changed.	*Levincia* Costs: 15,000
Miracle Seed		Boosts Grass-type moves.	*Mesagoza* Costs: 3,000
Mirror Herb		Mirror an opponent's stat increase once.	*Cascarrafa* Costs: 30,000
Misty Seed		Boosts Sp. Def on misty terrain once.	*Cascarrafa* Costs: 20,000
Muscle Band		Boosts the power of physical moves.	*Mesagoza* Costs: 8,000
Mystic Water		Boosts Water-type moves.	*Mesagoza* Costs: 3,000
Never-Melt Ice		Boosts Ice-type moves.	*Levincia* Costs: 3,000
Normal Gem		Boosts Normal-types moves.	*Cascarrafa* Costs: 15,000
Poison Barb		Boosts Poison-type moves.	*Cascarrafa* Costs: 3,000
Power Herb		Use a move that required a turn to charge up.	*Cascarrafa* Costs: 30,000
Protective Pads		Protects from effects triggered from direct contact moves.	*Levincia* Costs: 15,000

Item Name	Icon	Description	Location/Cost
Psychic Seed		Boosts Sp. Def on Psychic terrain once.	Cascarrafa Costs: 20,000
Punching Glove		Boosts punching-based moves by 50%	Mesagoza Costs: 15,000
Quick Claw		May let you move first.	Mesagoza Costs: 8,000
Razor Claw		Raises chance of a critical hit.	Mesagoza Costs: 15,000
Red Card		When hit, the attacker is removed from the battle.	Levincia Costs: 30,000
Ring Target		Moves that normally don't effect, now will.	Levincia Costs: 10,000
Rocky Helmet		If holder is hit, so too now is the attacker.	Mesagoza Costs: 50,000
Room Service		Lowers your speed during *Trick Room*.	Levincia Costs: 20,000
Safety Goggles		Protects you from weather and powder related damage.	Levincia Costs: 20,000
Scope Lens		Boosts your critical hit stats.	Levincia Costs: 15,000
Sharp Beak		Boosts Flying-type moves.	Mesagoza Costs: 3,000
Shed Shell		Guaranteed switch out.	Cascarrafa Costs: 20,000

Item Name	Icon	Description	Location/Cost
Shell Bell		Recovers some HP after every hit landed.	*Levincia* Costs: 20,000
Silk Scarf		Boosts Normal-type moves.	*Mesagoza* Costs: 3,000
Silver Powder		Boosts Bug-type moves.	*Mesagoza* Costs: 3,000
Smooth Rock		Extends the duration of the *Sandstorm* move	*Cascarrafa* Costs: 8,000
Snowball		Boosts Att stat if holder is hit with an Ice-type move.	*Cascarrafa* Costs: 5,000
Soft Sand		Boosts Ground-type moves.	*Levincia* Costs: 3,000
Spell Tag		Boosts Ghost-type moves.	*Cascarrafa* Costs: 3,000
Sticky Barb		Damages holder every turn, also damages targets that touch it.	*Levincia* Costs: 10,000
Terrain Extender		Boosts duration of terrain caused by a move or Ability.	*Cascarrafa* Costs: 15,000
Throat Spray		Raises Sp. Atk when using a sound-based move.	*Mesagoza* Costs: 20,000
Toxic Orb		Poisons the holder.	*Levincia* Costs: 15,000
Twisted Spoon		Boosts Psychic-type moves.	*Levincia* Costs: 3,000

Item Name	Icon	Description	Location/Cost
Utility Umbrella		Protects from weather effects.	*Cascarrafa* Costs: 15,000
Weakness Policy		Att and Sp. Atk boosted if user is hit with a move it is weak to.	*Mesagoza* Costs: 50,000
White Herb		Restores a lowered stat.	*Cascarrafa* Costs: 20,000
Wide Lens		Slightly boosts move accuracy.	*Levincia* Costs: 20,000
Wise Glasses		Boosts special moves power.	*Mesagoza* Costs: 8,000
Zoom Lens		Accuracy is boosted if user moves after target moves.	*Levincia* Costs: 10,000

Vitamins & Feathers

Item Name	Icon	Description
Calcium		Boosts Sp. Atk EV by 10, boost happiness.
Carbos		Boosts Speed EV by 10, boost happiness.
Clever Feather		Slightly boosts Sp. Def stats.
Genius Feather		Slightly boosts Sp. Atk stats.
Health Feather		Slightly boosts HP stats.
Iron		Boosts Def EV by 10, boost happiness.
Muscle Feather		Slightly boosts Attack stats.
Protein		Boosts Attack EV by 10, boost happiness.
Resist Feather		Slightly boosts Def stats.
Swift Feather		Slightly boosts Speed stats.
Zinc		Boosts Sp. Def EV by 10, boost happiness.

Item Name	Icon	Description
PP Up		Slightly boosts PP of a single move.
HP Up		Slightly boosts HP stat.

Medicine

Item Name	Icon	Description
Potion		Restores 20 HP.
Antidote		Cures poison status.
Burn Heal		Cures burn status.
Ice Heal		Removes frozen status.
Awakening		Removes sleep status.
Paralyze Heal		Free a paralyzed Pokémon.
Full Restore		Restores all HP and cures all status ailments.

Item Name	Icon	Description
Max Potion		Restores all HP.
Hyper Potion		Restores 120 HP.
Super Potion		Restores 60 HP
Full Heal		Removes all statuses once.
Revive		Revive one fainted Pokémon with half HP.
Max Revive		Revive one fainted Pokémon with full HP.
Fresh Water		Restores 30 HP.
Lemonade		Restores 70 HP.
Energy Powder		Restores 60 HP.
Energy Root		Restores 120 HP.

Item Name	Icon	Description
Heal Powder		Clears one status ailment.
Revival Herb		Revive one fainted Pokémon with some HP.
Soda Pop		Restores 50 HP.
Ether		Restore 10PP to a chosen move.
Max Ether		Fully restore all PP to a chosen move.
Elixir		Restores 10PP to all known moves.
Max Elixir		Restores all PP to all known moves.

Bug-Type TMs

Item Name	Icon	Description
Bug Buzz		Bug-type attack that can also lower a target's Sp. Def stat.
Leech Life		Your HP is restored by up-to half the damage taken by the target.
Pollen Puff		Use on a target to damage, use on an ally to restore its HP.
Pounce		Attacks and lower their Speed stat.
Struggle Bug		Attacks and lower their Sp. Atk stat.
U-turn		Attacks then switches with a Pokémon that's waiting.
X-Scissor		Attack that uses Scythes.

Dark-Type TMs

Item Name	Icon	Description
Crunch		Attack can lower target's Def stat.
Dark Pulse		Attack can also cause flinch.
Fake Tears		Attacks and harshly lower the their Sp. Def stat.
Fling		Throws your current item at your target. Damage is item dependent.
Foul Play		Turns the target's strength against it. The higher *their* Att stat, the more damage caused.
Nasty Plot		Sharply boosts your Sp. Atk stat.
Snarl		Lowers an enemy's Sp. Atk.
Taunt		Causes enemy to only use attacking moves for three turns.
Thief		Attacks and can steal an item (if they're not holding an item already).

Dragon-Type TMs

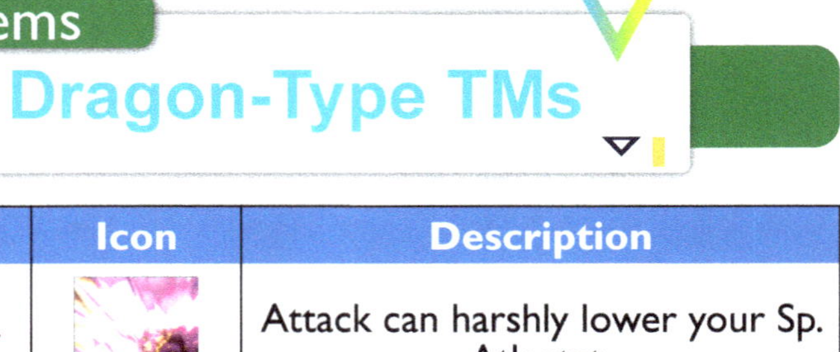

Item Name	Icon	Description
Draco Meteor		Attack can harshly lower your Sp. Atk stat.
Dragon Claw		Slash attack.
Dragon Dance		Boosts your Att and Speed stats.
Dragon Pulse		Dragon-type attack.
Dragon Tail		Target is swapped out. Single enemy fights end.
Outrage		Rampage attack for two to three turns, you then become confused.

Electric-Type TMs

Item Name	Icon	Description
Charge Beam		Attacks and boosts your Sp. Atk stat.
Eerie Impulse		Harshly lowers the target's Sp. Atk stat.
Electric Terrain		Electrifies ground for five turns. Ground-based Pokémon can't fall asleep.
Electro Ball		The faster you are, the more damage that is caused.
Thunder		Can cause paralysis.
Thunder Fang		Attacks and flinch, or leave it with paralysis.
Thunder Punch		Can cause paralysis.
Thunder Wave		Paralyzing Electric-type attack.
Thunderbolt		Electric-type attack that can cause paralysis.

Item Name	Icon	Description
Volt Switch		Attacks and then auto-switch Pokémon.
Wild Charge		Regular attack.

Fairy-Type TMs

Item Name	Icon	Description
Charm		Attacks and harshly lower their Attack stat.
Dazzling Gleam		Emits a powerful flash.
Disarming Voice		Causes emotional damage. Never misses.
Draining Kiss		Your HP is restored by over half of the damage taken by your target.
Misty Terrain		Protects Pokémon on the ground from status conditions, halves dragon-type damage for five moves.
Play Rough		Attack that can lower target's Att stat.

Fighting-Type TMs

Item Name	Icon	Description
Aura Sphere		Attack that never misses.
Body Press		The higher your defense stat, the greater the damage caused.
Brick Break		Attacks and also break barriers, such as 'Light Screen' and 'Reflect'.
Bulk Up		Boosts your Att and Def stats.
Close Combat		Attack that can also lower both your Def and Sp. Def stats.
Drain Punch		Attack causes your HP to be restored by up-to half the damage caused.
Focus Blast		Attack that can lower the target's Sp. Def stat.
Low Kick		Attacks and can knock heavier targets over.
Low Sweep		Attacks and lower their Speed stat.
Reversal		The lower your HP, the stronger the attack is.

Fire-Type TMs

Item Name	Icon	Description
Blast Burn		Causes damage and prevents you moving for turn two.
Fire Blast		Causes damage and sometimes also burn.
Fire Fang		Attacks and can cause flinch, or leave it with burns.
Fire Pledge		Fire-type attack. Can be combined with *Grass Pledge* to boost damage.
Fire Punch		Fire-type attack that can cause burn.
Fire Spin		Can cause fire damage for up to five turns.
Flame Charge		Attacks and boost your Speed stat.
Flamethrower		Fire-type attack that can cause burn.
Flare Blitz		Fire-type attack that can cause you damage and burn the target.

Item Name	Icon	Description
Heat Wave		Fire-type attack that can cause burn.
Sunny Day		Fire-based attacks are boosted for five turns. Also lowers the power of Water-type attacks.
Overheat		Attack that also lowers harshly lowers your Sp. Atk stats.
Will-O-Wisp		This attack causes burn.

Flying-Type TMs

Item Name	Icon	Description
Acrobatics		Can cause massive damage if the enemy isn't currently holding an item.
Aerial Ace		Damages the enemy. This attack never misses.
Air Cutter		Attacks and may land a critical hit.
Air Slash		The user attacks with a blade of air that slices even the sky. This may also make the target flinch.
Brave Bird		An attack that can also cause you damage.
Fly		Fly up on turn one, attack on turn two.
Hurricane		Flying-type attack that can also confuse the target.
Tailwind		Boost your whole team's Speed stat for four turns.

Ghost-Type TMs

Item Name	Icon	Description
Confuse Ray		Attacks and can cause confuse.
Hex		Causes additional damage to targets already afflicted with a status ailment.
Night Shade		Causes damage equal to your current level.
Phantom Force		Disappear for first turn, then land a strike on the second.
Shadow Ball		Attack can lower target's Sp. Def stat.
Shadow Claw		Attacks and may land a critical hit.

Grass-Type TMs

Item Name	Icon	Description
Bullet Seed		Can cause two to five hits in a row.
Energy Ball		Attack can lower target's Sp. Def stat.
Frenzy Plant		Grass-type attack that prevents you moving for turn two.
Giga Drain		Your HP is restored by up to half the target's damage.
Grass Knot		Grass-type attack. Affects heavier targets more.
Grass Pledge		Grass-type attack. Can be combined with *Water Pledge* to boost damage.
Grassy Terrain		Turns ground into grass for five turns. Restores HP of team on the ground and powers up Grass moves.
Leaf Storm		Grass-type attack that can also harshly lower your Sp. Atk stat.
Magical Leaf		This attack never misses.

Item Name	Icon	Description
Seed Bomb		Attacks from above with seeds.
Solar Beam		This attack won't happen until turn two.
Trailblaze		Attacks and boosts your Speed stat.

Items

Ground-Type TMs

Item Name	Icon	Description
Bulldoze		Attacks and lower the Speed stat of afflicted enemies.
Dig		Burrows underground for first turn, attacks on the second turn.
Drill Run		Attack can land a critical hit.
Earth Power		Ground-type attack that can lower target's Sp. Def stat.
Earthquake		Ground-type attack that can damage all targets at once.
Mud Shot		Attacks and lower their Speed stat.

Item Name	Icon	Description
Mud-Slap		Inflicts damage and lowers enemy accuracy.
Spikes		Damages Pokémon that switch in.
Stomping Tantrum		Attack power is doubled if your previous attack failed.

Items

Ice-Type TMs

Item Name	Icon	Description
Avalanche		Damage caused is double if the target has hurt you on the same turn.
Blizzard		Ice-type attack, can leave a target frozen.
Ice Beam		Ice-type attack that can leave a target frozen.
Ice Fang		Attacks and flinch, or leave it frozen.
Ice Punch		Ice-type attack that can freeze the target.
Ice Spinner		Ice-type attack.

Item Name	Icon	Description
Icy Wind	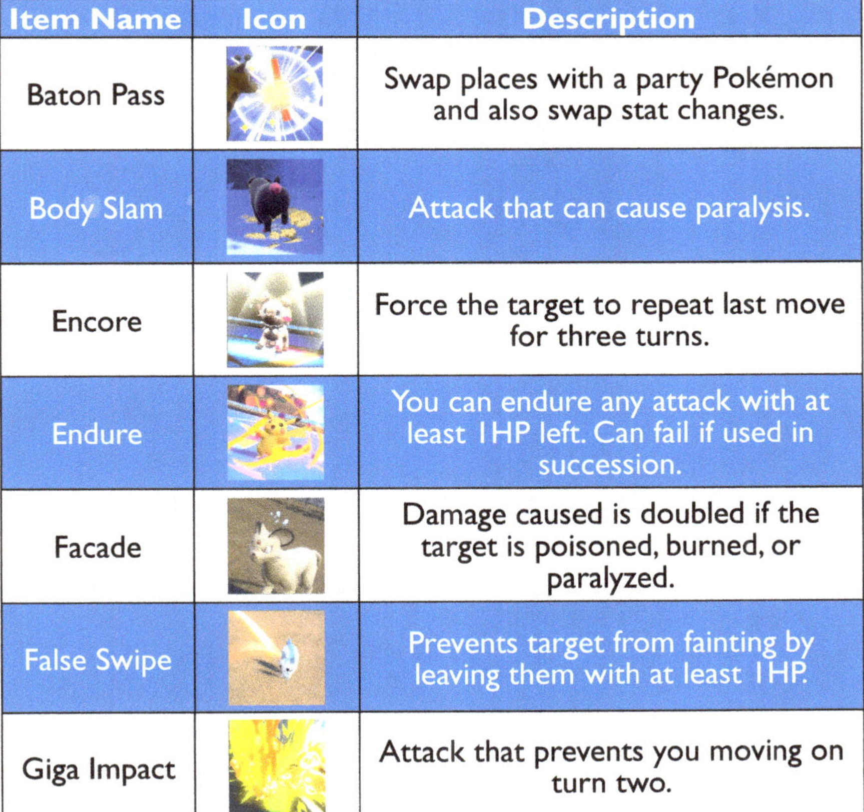	Can cause ice damage and lower their Speed stat.
Snowscape		Summon a snowstorm that lasts five turns. Also boosts Ice-type Def stats.

Normal-Type TMs

Item Name	Icon	Description
Baton Pass		Swap places with a party Pokémon and also swap stat changes.
Body Slam		Attack that can cause paralysis.
Encore		Force the target to repeat last move for three turns.
Endure		You can endure any attack with at least 1HP left. Can fail if used in succession.
Facade		Damage caused is doubled if the target is poisoned, burned, or paralyzed.
False Swipe		Prevents target from fainting by leaving them with at least 1HP.
Giga Impact		Attack that prevents you moving on turn two.

Item Name	Icon	Description
Helping Hand		Boosts power of an ally's attack.
Hyper Beam		Attack that also prevents you from moving on your next turn.
Hyper Voice		Normal-type attack.
Metronome		Causes you to use almost any move.
Scary Face		Attacks and harshly lower their speed stat.
Sleep Talk		Uses a known move at random whilst it is asleep.
Substitute		Sacrifices some HP to create a decoy in battle.
Swift		Attacks and lowers their Speed stat.
Swords Dance		Sharply boosts your Att stats.
Tera Blast		Only works if Terrastallized. Uses Atk or Sp.Atk.

Poison-Type TMs

Item Name	Icon	Description
Acid Spray		Attacks and harshly lower their Sp. Def stat.
Gunk Shot		Shoots garbage.
Poison Jab		Attack that can poison the target.
Poison Tail		Attacks, land a critical hit, and cause poison.
Sludge Bomb		Poison-type attack.
Toxic Spikes		Causes poison damage to Pokémon that switch in.
Venoshock		Inflict a poisonous attack. Doubles in strength when used on already poisoned targets.

Psychic-Type TMs

Item Name	Icon	Description
Agility		Sharply boosts its Speed stat.
Amnesia		Sharply boosts your Sp. Def stat.
Calm Mind		Boosts your Sp. Atk and Sp. Def stats.
Imprison		Prevents target using a move you both know.
Light Screen		Reduces physical damage taken for five turns.
Psybeam		Attacks and can cause confuse.
Psychic		Can lower target's Sp. Def stat.
Psychic Fangs		Attacks and also break barriers, such as 'Light Screen' and 'Reflect'.
Psychic Terrain		Protects Pokémon on the ground from priority moves and powers up Psychic moves for five turns.

Item Name	Icon	Description
Psyshock		Deals physical-type damage.
Reflect		Reduces physical damage taken for five turns.
Rest		Sleep for two turns. Cures status and restores all HP.
Skill Swap		Exchange abilities with the target.
Stored Power		Boosted stats stack to cause extra damage to the target.
Trick		Swap held items with the target.
Trick Room		Lets slower Pokémon move first for four to five turns.
Zen Headbutt		Attacks and can make the target flinch.

Rock-Type TMs

Item Name	Icon	Description
Power Gem		Attack that uses rays of light.
Rock Blast		Rock-type attack that hits two to five times in a row.
Rock Slide		Rock-type attack, can cause flinch.
Rock Tomb		Cause damage and lower their Speed stat.
Sandstorm		Restore up to half your max HP, regain more in a sandstorm.
Stealth Rock		Rock-type attack that damages target's who switch into battle.
Stone Edge		Attack that can land a critical hit.

Steel-Type TMs

Item Name	Icon	Description
Flash Cannon		Attack may also lower the target's Sp. Def stat.
Heavy Slam		The greater your weight vs. your target, the greater the damage caused.
Iron Defense		Boosts your Def stat.
Iron Head		Attack can also cause flinch.
Metal Claw		Attacks and may boost your Att stat.
Smart Strike		Attacks never miss.
Steel Beam		Steel-type attack that can also damage you.

Water-Type TMs

Item Name	Icon	Description
Chilling Water		Attacks and lower their Attack stat.
Hydro Cannon		The target is hit with a watery blast. The user can't move on the next turn.
Hydro Pump		Water-type attack.
Liquidation		Water-type Attack can lower target's Def stat.
Rain Dance		Water-based attacks that lasts for five turns. Also lowers the power of Fire-type attacks.
Surf		Attacks using a giant wave.
Water Pledge		Water-type attack. Can be combined with *Fire Pledge* to boost damage.
Water Pulse		Attacks and can cause confuse.
Waterfall		Charge at the target, may cause flinch.

Tera Shards

Item Name	Icon	Description
Bug Tera Shard		Exchange 50 in the Medali restaurant to change Tera Type to Bug.
Dark Tera Shard		Exchange 50 to change Tera Type to Dark.
Dragon Tera Shard		Exchange 50 to change Tera Type to Dragon.
Electric Tera Shard		Exchange 50 to change Tera Type to Electric.
Fairy Tera Shard		Exchange 50 to change Tera Type to Fairy.
Fighting Tera Shard		Exchange 50 to change Tera Type to Fighting.
Fire Tera Shard		Exchange 50 to change Tera Type to Fire.
Flying Tera Shard		Exchange 50 to change Tera Type to Flying.
Ghost Tera Shard		Exchange 50 to change Tera Type to Ghost.
Grass Tera Shard		Exchange 50 to change Tera Type to Grass.

Item Name	Icon	Description
Ground Tera Shard		Exchange 50 to change Tera Type to Ground.
Ice Tera Shard		Exchange 50 to change Tera Type to Ice.
Normal Tera Shard		Exchange 50 in the Medali restaurant to change Tera Type to Normal.
Poison Tera Shard		Exchange 50 to change Tera Type to Poison.
Psychic Tera Shard		Exchange 50 to change Tera Type to Psychic.
Rock Tera Shard		Exchange 50 to change Tera Type to Rock.
Steel Tera Shard		Exchange 50 to change Tera Type to Steel.
Water Tera Shard		Exchange 50 to change Tera Type to Water.

Evolution Items

Item Name	Icon	Description
Auspicious Armor		Evolves: Charcadet *into* Armarouge
Black Augurite		Evolves: Scyther *into* Kleavor
Dawn Stone		Evolves: Male Kirlia *into* Gallade, Female Snorunt *into* Froslass
Dusk Stone		Evolves Scyther *into* Kleavor
Fire Stone		Evolves: Vulpix *into* Ninetales, Growlithe *into* Arcanine, Eevee *into* Flareon, Pansear *into* Simisear, Capsakid *into* Scovillain
Galarica Cuff		Evolves: Slowpoke *into* Slowbro
Galarica Wreath		Evolves: Slowpoke *into* Slowking

Item Name	Icon	Description
Ice Stone		Evolves: Vulpix *into* Ninetales, Sandshrew *into* Sandslash, Eevee *into* Glaceon, Darumaka *into* Darmanitan, Crabrawler *into* Crabominable, Cetoddle *into* Cetitan
King's Rock		Evolves: Poliwhirl *into* Politoed, Slowpoke *into* Slowking
Leader's Crest		Evolves: Bisharp *into* Kingambit
Leaf Stone		Evolves: Gloom *into* Vileplume, Weepinbell *into* Victreebel, Voltorb *into* Electrode, Exeggcute *into* Exeggutor, Eevee *into* Leafeon, Nuzleaf *into* Shiftry, Pansage *into* Simisage
Malicious Armor		Evolves: Charcadet *into* Ceruledge

Item Name	Icon	Description
Metal Coat		Evolves: Onix *into* Steelix, Scyther *into* Scizor
Moon Stone		Evolves: Nidorina *into* Nidoqueen, Nidorino *into* Nidoking, Clefairy *into* Clefable, Jigglypuff *into* Wigglytuff, Skitty *into* Delcatty, Munna *into* Musharna
Razor Claw		Evolves: Sneasel *into* Weavile
Scroll of Darkness		Evolves: Kubfu *into* Urshifu
Scroll of Waters		Evolves: Kubfu *into* Urshifu
Shiny Stone		Evolves: Togetic *into* Togekiss, Roselia *into* Roserade, Minccino *into* Cinccino, Orange Floette *into* Orange Florges

Item Name	Icon	Description
Sun Stone		Evolves: Gloom *into* Bellossom, Sunkern *into* Sunflora, Cottonee *into* Whimsicott, Petilil *into* Lilligant, Helioptile *into* Heliolisk
Sweet Apple		Evolves: Applin *into* Appletun
Tart Apple		Evolves: Applin *into* Flapple
Thunder Stone		Evolves: Pikachu *into* Raichu, Magneton *into* Magnezone, Eevee *into* Jolteon, Eelektrik *into* Eelektross, Charjabug *into* Vikavolt, Tadbulb *into* Bellibolt
Water Stone		Evolves: Poliwhirl *into* Poliwrath, Shellder *into* Cloyster, Staryu *into* Starmie, Eevee *into* Vaporeon

Sandwich Fillings

Item Name	Icon	Description
Avocado		A sweet and tasty ingredient.
Apple		Very sweet fruit.
Bacon		A salty and tasty ingredient.
Banana		Very sweet, Pokémon love it
Basil		Very bitter, fragrant & versatile.
Baguette		A long loaf sliced into top and bottom halves.
Bitter Herb Mystica		An *extremely* bitter condiment.
Butter		Use to evolve Grass-types.
Cheese		Very salty, used in sandwiches.
Cherry Tomato		A very tart ingredient.
Chili Sauce		Extremely spicy with a kick.

Item Name	Icon	Description
Chorizo		A very salty and spicy ingredient.
Cream Cheese		Very sweet and tart flavor.
Cucumber		A tart & bitter ingredient.
Curry Powder		Very spicy condiment.
Egg		Lightly salty ingredient.
Fried Fillet		Salty & bitter. Pair with sour.
Green B Pepper		A slightly bitter ingredient.
Ham		A very salty ingredient.
Hamburger		Very salty and filling to eat.
Herbed Sausage		A very salty and bitter sausage.
Horseradish		Very spicy condiment.
Jalapeno		**Very** spicy.
Jam		Both very sweet and very sour.

Item Name	Icon	Description
Ketchup		A very salty and tart condiment.
Kiwi		Very tart fruit, little sweet.
Klawf Stick		A very sweet and salty ingredient.
Lettuce		A bitter tasting ingredient.
Marmalade		Sour and bitter condiment.
Mayonnaise		Packs a very tart punch.
Mustard		A spicy condiment (try with Ketchup...)
Noodles		Salty ingredient.
Olive Oil		Sour and bitter condiment.
Onion		Use to evolve Water-types.
Peanut Butter		A very sweet condiment.
Pepper		Very spicy seasoning.
Pickle		A very sour ingredient.

Item Name	Icon	Description
Pineapple		Fruit, cut into chunks.
Potato Salad		Very tart, works well with bread.
Potato Tortilla		Very salty and popular.
Prosciutto		Very salty (like regular ham).
Red Bell Pepper		A slightly bitter ingredient.
Red Onion		A slightly sweet ingredient.
Rice		Lightly sweet ingredient.
Salt		A very salty seasoning.
Salty Herb Mystica		Legendarily salty condiment.
Smoked Fillet		Very salty, bitter, and smoked.
Sour Herb Mystica		Extremely sour condiment.
Spicy Herb Mystica		The mightiest of all spices.
Strawberry		Very sweet and tart fruit.

Item Name	Icon	Description
Sweet Herb Mystica		Extremely sweet condiment.
Tofu		Lightly sweet ingredient.
Tomato		A very tart ingredient.
Vinegar		Very sour condiment.
Wasabi		Spicy and similar to horseradish.
Watercress		Very bitter with a quirky flavor.
Whipped Cream		Very sweet condiment.
Yellow Bell Pepper		A slightly bitter ingredient.
Yogurt		Both very sweet and sour.

Hidden Treasure
2-Part Premium DLC

Announced in February 2023, Pokémon Scarlet & Violet will be receiving single-player DLC, known as *The Hidden Treasure of Area* Zero, that's being released as two separate parts:

- *Part 1: The Teal Mask*
- *Part 2: The Indigo Disk*

This DLC can be pre-ordered now from within the main menu in the game.

The DLC isn't included as part of the Nintendo Online Subscription service (at least at the time of writing this in March 2023).

This means you must pay for it to unlock the DLC.

Pre-Order Bonuses

If you pre-order the game before the end of October 2023, then you'll be granted access to two bonuses:

1. *A selection of season-themed clothing (see the pictures opposite for examples of what they look like).*

Note

The contents of the new Uniform Set differs between the Scarlet and Violet versions of the game.

2. *A Lvl. 50 Zoroark that comes with a Dark-type TT, a Charismatic Mark, and the Normal-type move: Happy Hour.*

Caution

The code provided to download the *Zoroark* can only be used **once** AND it is committed to that particular save file!

MAIN MENU
Bag
Boxes
Picnic
Poké Portal
Options
Save
Downloadable Content

DLC Part I
The Teal Mask (by Dec 2023)

What we know so far...

This adventure occurs on the land of *Kitakami*, and you've been chosen as one of the students who must take part in a school trip that's held each year.

Kitakami is a place of large mountains and tranquility. Your trip coincides with a festival that's happening in the village, so expect to meet loads of new NPC characters and Trainers to battle.

The Legendary Ogerpon

This legendary green Pokémon dons a fearsome mask.

The Heroes of Kitakami

There are three Pokémon that are renowned throughout.

Munkidori

The blue and black monkey that likely has a few cheeky tricks up its furry sleeves.

Okidogi

A large dog-like Pokemon who's bite may well be as big as its bark...

Fezandipiti

Don't let this elegant **Flying-type** Pokémon fool you. It has some sharp claws that will likely cause you some *serious* damage if you're not prepared!

It's more than likely that these Pokémon will be epic battles, so we're really looking forward to battling them and adding them to our collection at the end of the year!

DLC Part 2

Indigo Disk (by April 2024)

What we know so far...

Part two takes you on a trip as an exchange student to your academy's sister-school - The Blueberry Academy.

As with your own academy, this school absolutely *loves* Pokémon battling.

However, what's not common knowledge is the fact that this academy is located **underwater!!!**

The Legendary Terapagos

This glittering Pokémon looks amazing and the type-symbols all over its back would indicate that it may well present itself as quite a challenge in the final part of this DLC adventure.

Familiar Pokémon coming to Scarlet & Violet

We've been promised that over 230 familiar Pokémon will be available to play (which includes any Pokémon that you transfer using Pokémon HOME or via trades.

Nintendo have yet to reveal which Pokémon are you be available.

However, on the official website, the left-hand picture on the next page was labelled as "Mask" in the filename and the right-hand picture was labelled "Disk").

We're looking forward to seeing what's revealed next!

Also Available
From Alpha Strategy Guides

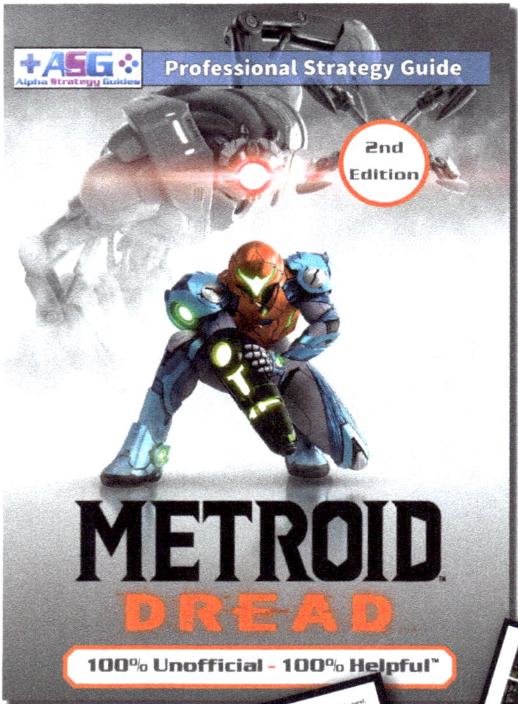

Our redesigned Metroid Dread strategy guide provides you with expert strategies from a veteran Metroid player.

Defeat every boss, master every move, locate every Missile pack, E-Tank, Power Bomb, and suit upgrade.

Break the game wide open with intentional and unintentional sequence breaks, speedruns, and a whole lot more!

Available now!

Alpha Strategy Guides presents the 3rd Edition of the No. 1 selling unofficial strategy guide to Link's Awakening, also on the Switch.

Our guide helps you to overcome every challenge, defeat every enemy and boss, locate every secret (including every Heart Piece and Secret Seashell), hidden Easter Eggs, and a whole lot more.

Available now!

The classic Metroid Prime got an unexpected remaster in February 2023.

Our comprehensive guide, authored by a veteran Metroid Prime master, not only shows you how to beat every boss (on Hard difficulty), collect every item, and obtain every scan, but it also shows you how to sequence break the game and enter its legendary "Secret Wolds".

You *definitely* won't want to miss this guide…

Available March 2023.

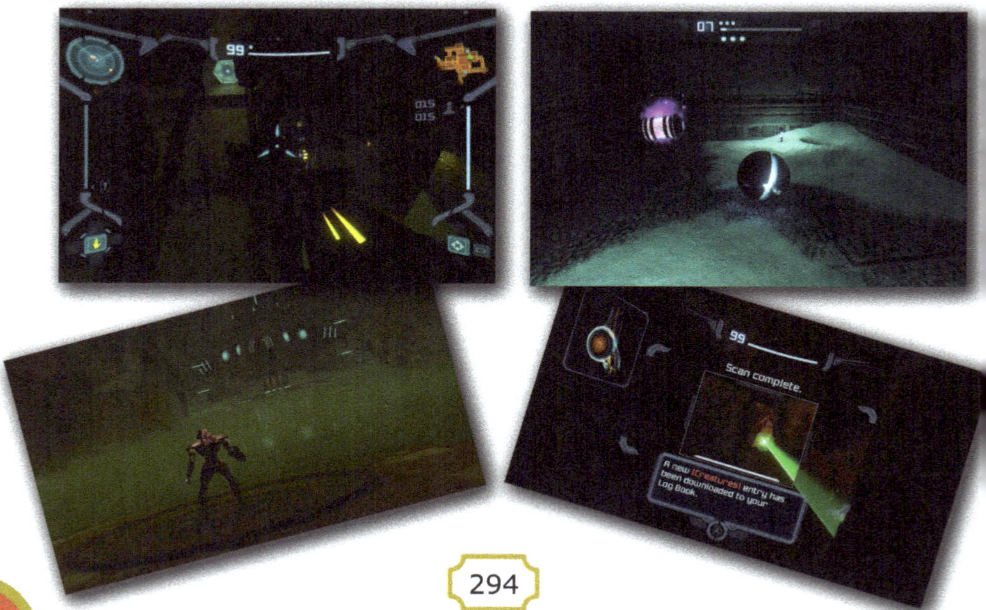

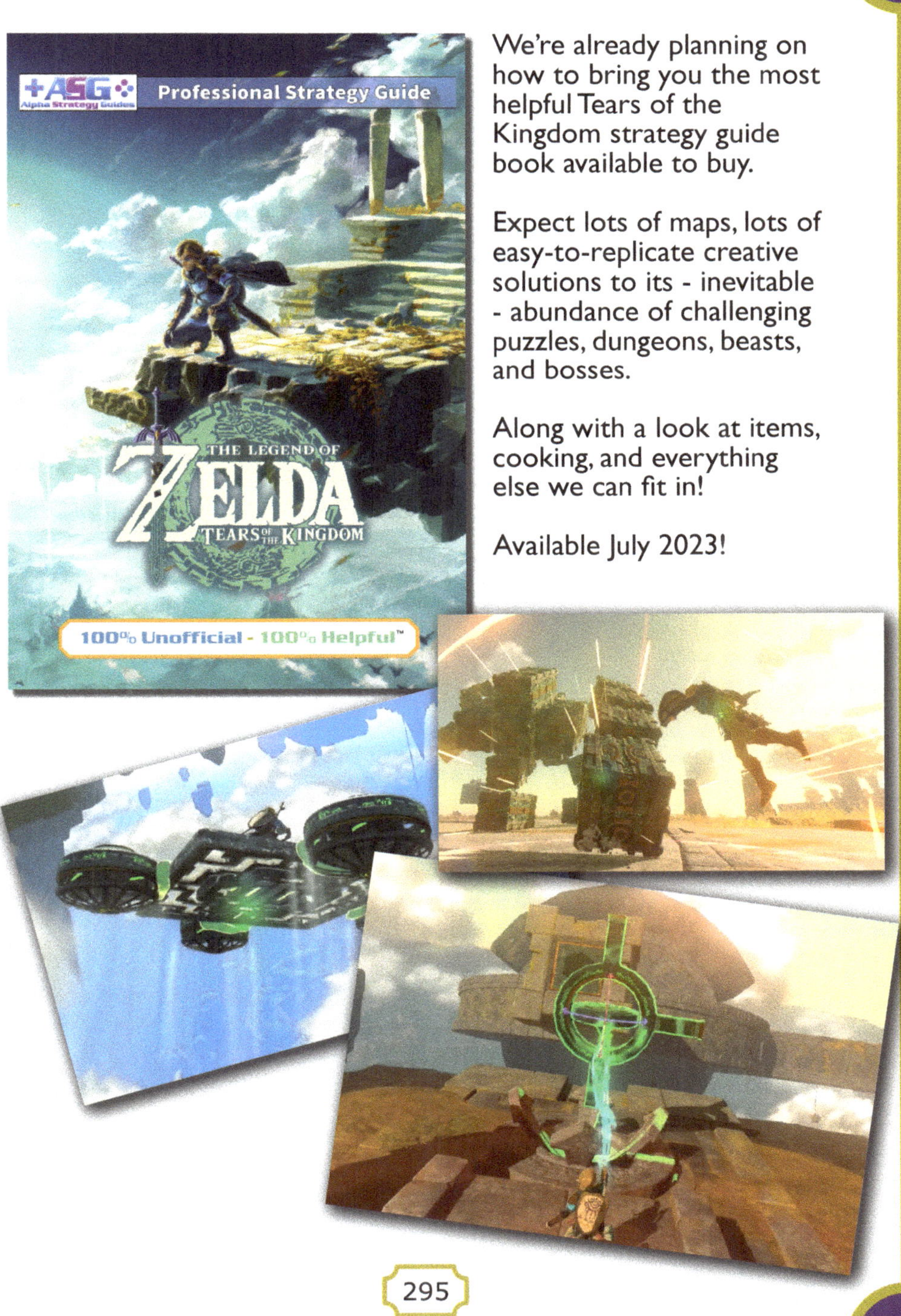

We're already planning on how to bring you the most helpful Tears of the Kingdom strategy guide book available to buy.

Expect lots of maps, lots of easy-to-replicate creative solutions to its - inevitable - abundance of challenging puzzles, dungeons, beasts, and bosses.

Along with a look at items, cooking, and everything else we can fit in!

Available July 2023!

Thank you for reading!

Please don't forget to leave a review. We genuinely read them all and take all suggestions into consideration.

Best wishes,

The Alpha Strategy Guides team.

www.ingramcontent.com/pod-product-compliance
Lightning Source LLC
LaVergne TN
LVHW082159060425
807891LV00010B/192